Psycholinguistics

*Experiments in
Spontaneous Speech*

Psycholinguistics

Experiments in Spontaneous Speech

F. GOLDMAN EISLER

Psycholinguistics Research Unit
Department of Phonetics
University College, London, England

1968

ACADEMIC PRESS
LONDON AND NEW YORK

ACADEMIC PRESS INC. (LONDON) LTD.
24/28 Oval Road
London NW1

U.S. Edition published by
ACADEMIC PRESS INC.
111 Fifth Avenue
New York, New York 10003

Library of Congress Catalog Card Number: 68-24697
SBN: 12 289250 X

PRINTED IN GREAT BRITAIN BY
THE WHITEFRIARS PRESS LTD., LONDON AND TONBRIDGE

Preface

The purpose of writing this book was two-fold. The research which I have been carrying out since the early fifties is reported in papers which are spread over a variety of journals, reaching different groups of readers. To make this work available to the interested reader it had to be presented in one volume. In addition, it seemed desirable to bring out some of the wider theoretical implications which seemed, in my view, to evolve as the evidence from these investigations accumulated.

This research was made possible through the generous support of two institutions. During the initial period lasting from 1950 to 1958 the research was carried out under the auspices of the Medical Research Council, London, while its extension and further development from 1958 onwards was made possible by the National Institutes of Health, Bethesda, Maryland. I herewith wish to express to these bodies my appreciation for having enabled me to pursue a line of investigation which when it started led into an uncharted territory and whose novelty held uncertain promise.

Psycholinguistics was neither name nor concept at the time and the few workers who busied themselves in this area were very much on their own and cut off from the main stream of psychological interest. In this situation the home which Prof. D. B. Fry offered me in the Department of Phonetics at University College London in 1955 together with his continued interest and encouragement were ample compensation for the aloofness with which most psychologists regarded the subject of language and speech.

This situation has changed dramatically in the last few years and even extralinguistic phenomena, still very much less a favourite than linguistic phenomena proper, are now receiving the attention of psychological experimentalists.

A considerable body of work is now in existence of which we owe systematic reviews to George F. Mahl and G. Schultze (Psychological Research in the Extralinguistic Area, "Approaches to Semantics" edited by T. A. Sebeok et al., Monton & Co., The Hague, 1964) and to S. Ervin-Tripp and D. I. Slobin (Psycholinguistics, *Annual Review of Psychology* **17**, 435, 1966).

If no reference to this body of work was made in this book it is because by the time these studies appeared my own initial gropings had gained momentum and were drawn on by their own logic. I therefore confined myself to reporting my own research and the work of those who closely collaborated with me. I have made reference in the text to sources which were immediately relevant but the debt owed to some writers cannot be pinpointed in any particular context. These writers include Henri Bergson, Claude Bernard, Ernst Cassirer, Henri Delacroix, Kurt Goldstein, Hughlings Jackson, Karl Lashley, Luria, Monakov, Sechenov, Heinz Werner, Wundt. If their varied and profound contributions permit a reduction to a common denominator it seems that all of them support the view of language and speech as a dynamic process and as an organic part of the psychobiological totality of the development and behaviour of man.

I further wish to thank my colleague Dr. Peter Wason who read the manuscript and did his best to curb my predilection for writing long sentences.

Last but not the least of my debts in gratitude belongs to my subjects, in particular to my colleagues of the Department of Phonetics, University College London, who took part in some of the most time-consuming experiments, and to the professional conference interpreters who gave generously of their time in experiments, of which only some aspects are reported here.

March, 1968   *F. Goldman Eisler*

Contents

The Problem

In 1948 I was employed by the Medical Research Council with an assignment for making a study of the technique of interviewing. The need for a more systematic understanding of this procedure than was available had for some time been felt by workers using and having to rely on this method for social investigation, for assessment of personnel and personality and for diagnosis and treatment in psychiatry. At the same time the prospects of a solution of this problem in terms of experimental control were poor, because spontaneity is the very essence and virtue of interviewing. Indeed an interviewer's ability to manipulate it in accordance with his aim, and his flexibility in making use of feedback supplied through the dialogue and the interpersonal contact, is the key to his success. Whatever attempts had been made to increase the reliability and validity of interviewing through forms of standardization and control the logic of the situation admitted only one conclusion: namely that interviewing, i.e. engaging another person in conversation with a certain aim in view, as indeed any conversation between two people, required the kind of contact in which each in the dialogue was nourished by the feedback received from the partner. Whether this step was an exchange as in normal conversation, or a question, a probe or prompting as might be an interviewer's contribution, it would miss being appropriate without continuous feedback. Therefore, interference with the spontaneity of this process through standardization must be unacceptable to just those interviewers who were most successful in adjusting to the subtle nuances revealed in such contact.

Such interviewers operate as artists and craftsmen do, unwilling and, because their exercise is largely intuitive, unable to accept the strictures of techniques of standardization derived from alien methods such as questionnaires and tests. More consistent were those workers who, despairing of ever being able to bring order into what seemed a chaotic situation, proposed to divide the function of the interview between tests and questionnaires for eliciting information on the one hand, and conditioning for modifying and manipulating people's behaviour and responses on the other. Thus a situation was arrived at which is characteristic of the position of psychology at large. Living speech and language as used in spontaneous human communication was placed outside the pale of the legitimate area of psychological enquiry as

1

indeed were other creative pursuits of human beings.

Curiosity did not extend to what would have seemed a step consequent upon and leading to the understanding of such a situation, namely to the enquiry into what were the constituent elements of conversational activity and what were the patterns, if any, of their successive occurrence. The disinclination of experimental psychologists to analyse the complex of conversational behaviour or of such skills generally as involve temporal patterns is an intriguing phenomenon which deserves being examined more closely than can be done here in the light of the history of scientific psychology and the philosophy of science in general.

From the former we learn about the awareness in the early days of psychology of successiveness as a basic character of psychical life, about William James' "stream of consciousness", about "thought being a sensibly continuous stream". The persisting determining tendencies directing and integrating associative successions as conceived by the Wurzburg school and the theory of schema as proposed by Head show a similar vista. This conception was dimmed in subsequent development though even in his time William James complained that traditional psychology overlooked the "free water of consciousness" as if the stream was nothing but "pails or pots" full of water. The development of psychology in the direction of experiment and quantification had the same consequences for it as the transmutation of natural phenomena to numbers had brought to the physical sciences.

As Bergson pointed out (1912), this resulted in time giving place to space and in simultaneity taking over from duration, science having eliminated from its calculations the temporal element and substituted homogeneity, repetition and simultaneity for heterogeneity, continuity and succession. The consequence of this for psychology, however, is more serious than for the physical sciences. For time in its various manifestations as succession, continuity and duration is too basic a datum of experience to be left out of the psychological account. Concerning thinking, for example, to disregard the essentially evolutionary nature of the process, the continuous movement between images and meaning and from there to formulation, has sadly impoverished the scope of thought psychology. Yet it must be granted that duration, as pregnant a datum as it may be, is most elusive to observation. How indeed was James' suggestion (1890) that "the successive passing thoughts inherit each other's possessions" and also contain "premonitory perspective views of schemes of thought not yet articulate" to be examined by the objective methods that we nowadays insist on? And even the act of temporal integration, an indispensable condition of experience and a concept which was taken up by Hebb (1949), Lashley (1951) and Fessard (1954), has, in spite of what Lashley terms "the ubiquity of the problem", in his own words "been largely ignored". However, since the time when Lashley complained that "it [temporal integration] is not even mentioned in recent text-books, nor is there any significant body of experimental studies bearing on the problem", temporal phenomena have been paid more attention. The influence of cybernetics and information theory with their concepts of time series and temporal context, of sequential dependencies and of control through feedback, have added substance to Lashley's theories of temporal integration. But even as late as 1960 George Miller, Karl Pribram, *et al.* were exceptions among psychologists in appreciating the central importance of the attitude to time for planning and for the integration and co-ordination of the plans, individually and socially. George Miller pointed out that anthropologists have been more aware than psychologists of attitude to time and its fundamental role in planning. This certainly was borne out by the new approach to the analysis of interviews initiated by the anthropologist E. D. Chapple. His technique of measuring time sequences was the initial spur that prompted the work which is reported here. Although this soon branched into new avenues and my interest shifted from the interpersonal to the intrapersonal plane, successiveness has remained a central object of study.

Chapple (1940, 1942) was interested in the objective representation of attitudes to time in action and in progress, and in their measurement. He selected the duration of periods of speech and silence in interviews and their interaction as his variable, measured and related them in sequential order and derived cumulative curves representing their progress in time. By recording continuously the mutual effect of feedback as reflected in these measures, and the mutual adjustment of speakers in interaction, Chapple not only applied (at least implicitly) cybernetic dynamics in the form of a technique of measurement, but he also showed by such practice that it was not impossible to leave the shore from which we are used to watch the flow of time and to swim with the current without getting submerged, while continuously recording it (see Appendix I).

The efforts of man to rid himself of the domination of time have been much commented upon (Fraisse, 1964), and it has been said that by taking up the position of spectator at the shore we affirm our conquest of time and our liberation from its domination. We then treat time as a thing at our disposal—we have time, we lose time—not as something of which we are a part. But in conversation, in speech which is spread over time, we become subject to it again; we must operate in time and we must adjust to the time of our partner. In spontaneous conversation man's way of handling time is revealed and by studying his speech behaviour under these conditions we may comprehend his attitudes when time is his master, when, whatever else the wider purpose of interlocutors may be, their primary, inescapable object must be to participate in, if not to take possession of, time without which speech cannot take place. In conversation, time is a quantity to be shared between partners and the more spontaneous it is, the more open is left the manner in which this time for talking will be distributed between them. Each speaker's own time again must be organized to accommodate activities in the several systems which contribute to the production of speech.

What seemed the most promising aspect of measuring the duration of events in sequence was that by this method objective measurement and quantification of behaviour in progress could be achieved without breaking up its continuity and temporal pattern.

In using it I found that it was possible to distill from the spontaneous and free flow of conversations temporal patterns of considerable invariance. This brought an approach to personality within reach which by its combination of formal and temporal aspects opened paths to its understanding in terms of dynamic and physiological parameters. The division of time into periods of activity (speech) and inactivity (silence) proved particularly fruitful from this point of view and what emerged in the first place through studying the mutual relations of these quantities was that "the stable element in the time pattern of conversations of individuals is to be found, not so much in those measures which are concerned with their active behaviour, as in those belonging to the intervals of inactivity between the periods of action" (Goldman-Eisler, 1951). Tendencies for maintaining long periods of silence or holding up action at one extreme, or incapacity to do so and precipitate action at the other, were found to constitute a relatively permanent feature of individuals' conversational behaviour. Curiosity about periods of external inactivity was aroused. The technique of measuring on and off periods of speech, however, was now no more applied to the totality of exchanges between individuals in interaction, where silence is the period of the interlocutor talking, but to vocal action and silence of one person's output of continuous utterance. These periods of silence were shown to be the main determinants of the rate of speech (Goldman-Eisler, 1955) and this in turn emerged as a personality characteristic of remarkable constancy. Pauses interrupting the smooth flow of speech thus became the main subject of all further investigation. The question presenting itself was: if activity in conversation, if vocal action, is a peripheral phenomenon, might not absence of activity indicate the presence of central activity? A technique for studying the relation between speaking and thinking seemed to have been found. The study of behaviour had always been concerned with observable acts, but if we take the continuity of the individual for granted, if we consider that time cannot be contemplated as empty nor duration be without content, then we might be able to get behind the external appearance of in-activity. This pursuit and its results will be described in the chapters that follow.

Introduction

The specific aim of the experiments reported in this volume was to gain an understanding of the generative processes involved in the production of speech. The problem which started these investigations is old as well as common to all who wish to gauge the intentions, the significance and the true meaning not only of, but behind what a person says; it concerns all those, in other words, who have realized that there is more information to be got out of the act of speaking than the verbal content of the linguistic product. The intuitive interpretation of the so often intangible messages contained in the act of human communication is a practice in human relations at which some are more successful than others, but which nobody who lives in the society of others can afford to neglect.

The act of speaking consists of a chain of events which links physiological and logical operations, which runs the gamut from animal cry to symbolic expression and which launches somatic, unconscious and subconscious experience into consciousness. It uses organs the original function of which is to serve vital biological needs, such as breathing, eating and crying in emotion, but speech is, at the same time, not possible without the co-operation of the highest levels and latest organs of the nervous system. The complete speech act is a dynamic process, demanding the mobilization in proper sequence of a series of complex procedures and is the temporal integration of serial phenomena. It is a most articulate and most finely graded external projection of internal processes organized and integrated in time.

If we can learn to disentangle this pattern, to identify the various levels of the organism's activity in the different elements of language and speech, we may well find ourselves on the way to bridging the gap between psychology and its allied sciences, physiology, neurology and biochemistry.

A contemplation of the processes involved in the production of speech will show that this is a reasonable expectation. The speech act is the end product of a fusion of functions which, directly and indirectly, involve the entire body. The muscular walls of the torso, the muscles of the respiratory tract, the pharynx, the tongue, the lips and face, the nasal passageways and those parts of the cerebro-spinal system that control and monitor these organs constitute the speech apparatus. At the same time most of these organs and parts have many functions other than speech. Their primary function is to serve biologically vital needs such as the vegetative reactions of swallowing, gagging, breathing, vomiting, suckling or biting, chewing, sucking and the emotional reactions such as laughing, sobbing, smiling, grimacing. Beside these automatic re-actions, a number of voluntary reactions other than speech may com-pete for the service of these organs such as exploratory movements of the tongue, kissing, blowing, or such skills as whistling, humming a tune, or playing a wind instrument.

Human speech is thus achieved by turning to new use organs which were developed at an earlier stage of evolution for life-serving activities, without adapting them anatomically in any way. These organs continue to serve the original vital functions, and speech must therefore compete with these functions for the use of these organs. This it does through the exercise of voluntary control, for this extremely complex situation must lead to interferences, first by inhibiting the competetive vital functions and then by adjusting the functioning of these organs according to a programme of trained movements. The utterance of speech sounds is the result of the co-ordination of these movements. This means that although the same organs perform the operations of swallowing, gagging, vomit-ing, suckling, sucking, breathing, chewing, laughing or sobbing, etc.— as they do those of speaking—the former movements are activated at the cerebellar level whilst the movements of speech are controlled from the cortex.

Three groups of organs participate in the peripheral speech act of articulation:

(1) those with respiratory function involving lungs and diaphragm,
(2) those whose function is phonation involving the pharynx, larynx and the vocal chords
(3) and those whose function is articulation proper, involving the mouth and mouth cavity, the nasal passageways, lips, tongue, teeth and palate.

While in primitive cries and calls the air erupts unchecked from chest and lungs, in speech its free flow is halted and guided under control, while fast and skilful movements of lips, tongue, jaws, etc. manipulate it along palate and teeth, etc. to give it specific character and sound. The continuous stream of primitive sound is thus separated into highly controlled discrete elements of well defined and distinct structure easily to be recognized. By allotting these structures of sounds to experience, organized in different categories, the process of symbolic representation is completed. Speaking amounts to producing sequences of such distinct structures in such a way that they convey a message and a meaning. This property of being divisible into distinct units together with the properties of control, of following rules of grammatical integration, of sequential organization and expressiveness makes speech undoubtedly the most suitable area of human behaviour for the study and measurement of the productive processes and of the psychophysiological relationships which we must assume to be involved in their generation.

The units which compose the dynamic and semantic structure of speech belong to different classes of phenomena and to different systems of organization: (1) there are the linguistic systems concerned with phonemic, lexical and grammatical, i.e. syntactic, operations, (2) the physical, physiological and neuro-physiological systems, i.e. operating through respiratory, muscular and electrical activity, and (3) the temporal phenomena, which include durations of activity by any of these systems and of the gaps of inactivity which interrupt and alternate with activity.

Normal speech consists of series of well integrated structures of such units produced in rapid succession. Linguists and grammarians, whose prerogative the study of language has been until recent times, have based themselves on written language or written records of spoken language only. To them we owe a most imposing system of classification and analysis of vocabulary as well as grammar which puts at our disposal a whole range of relatively well defined linguistic categories and enables us to describe language in terms of quantities in the various categories and their relationships. This leaves out the live product, however, by separating it from the producer and his activity. It also concentrates on the normative and prescribed and gives no account of the actual speech performance, although recently some linguists have turned their interest to this area. This interest may be expected to increase since, through the technological advances in recording live speech, speaking as a spontaneous activity (i.e. undetached from its behavioural concomitants) has become accessible to detailed analysis. The sound recorder, having made available records of spoken language frozen into permanent form, enables us to subject the most spontaneous utterances of human beings produced under all, even the most natural and transitory, conditions to inspection, analysis and evaluation. Its information is not limited to the content and linguistics of utterances, but includes data about the manner in which these are produced, i.e. expressive features such as intonation, quality and intensity of voice, rhythm, stress, speed, hesitation, respiration, etc.

The divisibility of speech activity into units is therefore of more than theoretical interest. Once the whole process is made available for measurement, the quantitative analysis of the speech process as a dynamic entity has become a practical proposition.

The study of spontaneous speech is essential if the aim of the enquiry is to gain an understanding of the generative processes involved in speech production.

This becomes clear when we contemplate how the normal flow of speech masks the hierarchy of generative processes. It is revealed in aphasic dissociation, but in the flow of normal speech voluntary and automatic activities are closely interlaced, symbolic behaviour alternates with habitual verbalization, the construction of propositions with emotional expression and with the use of ready-made phrases, choice in fitting words to meaning takes turns with submission to the routine course and to the constraints of learned sequences, and abstract detachment in the use of word symbols gives way to concrete merging of situation and sign. The different processes involved and levels of control engaged fuse into a well-blended single phenomenon, so often described as stream of speech. This external picture of normal speech may be responsible for the monistic interpretations about the nature of encoding, such as the Markoff (1913) theory of speech, viewing it as a linear process, a left-to-right progression whereby each successive element is generated in accordance with transitional probabilities. However, a theory of this kind with its purely historical model of the sentence source and its concept of a finite sequence of elements generated from left to right is too simple to account for the facts of language. Chomsky (1957) made this point from his analysis of linguistic structure. It is only through the analysis of the act and the actuality of speaking, however, that we come to grips more directly with the workings of the processes which operate when speech is being generated. It is Hughlings Jackson's (1878) merit to have emphasized this dynamic relationship between brain processes and speech situation. The "same" utterance, he pointed out, which has become automatic and therefore well organized by being often used for symbolizing frequently presented things would become once more "voluntary speech" if it were used on a new occasion. When words are fitted to circumstances, when they symbolize a relation of things not already organized but being organized at the time of utterance, their use becomes voluntary. Hughlings Jackson's concept of "superior speech" is thus based on a functioning system of voluntary action. The distinctive feature is, in his view, not to be found in the utterance itself; it belongs to the process behind its production which may be gauged from the context of the speech.

Speech of this kind is best met when the utterance is spontaneous, when speakers are thinking on their feet, and it is in these conditions that one may expect the relationship between speaking and thinking to reveal itself most naturally.

Productivity becomes an event in the here and now of the speech act.

In normal speech, we must think of it as being embedded in a large mass of routine and therefore automatic verbal behaviour—only in the aphasic, the study of which led Hughlings Jackson to postulate the duality of speech, does this come to the surface and productivity is dissociated from habitual verbalization.

Normal spontaneous speech might be viewed as a highly integrated blend of processes at both levels where results of practice alternate with spontaneous creation.

The experiments reported here approached the distinction between the two different levels of speech generation in the first place as a problem of measurement, applied to spontaneous speech such as we meet in conversations, discussions and undirected interviews and verbal assignments which leave the subjects free in their choice of language. Such speech was chosen for study because here the speaker is organizing speech on the spur of the moment and is improvising and creating speech anew. Piecemeal linguistic productions evoked in the laboratory under controlled conditions must differ from continuous speech produced under conditions allowing for complete spontaneity in that they will lack the internal unity of signification such as distinguishes a gesture from a sum of movements (Merleau-Ponty, 1965).

It was because I wished to understand this signification of the gesture of spontaneous speech that, whatever controls were exercised over the situations which were to stimulate the production of speech, once launched, the discourse was left to follow a natural course. To trace the contour of natural speech behaviour it was necessary in the first place to see whether one might not be able to isolate, from the relatively smooth flow of spontaneous speech, elements that might prove to be indicative of the different levels of nervous activity involved in speech production.

Chapter 1

Some Facts Concerning Pauses in Speech

Speech is a serial phenomenon, an activity spread out in time. It does not, however, fill time continuously, particularly when it is spontaneous, but comes in fits and starts with intermittent periods of non-speech. A passage of speech extending into time consists of two sorts of time: time of vocal action and time of silence.

This is evident if the output on the magnetic tape on which such speech has been recorded is transformed into a visual record. This is done by feeding the output from a tape recorder through a signal detector which translates the signal from the tape recorder into pulses co-extensive in time with the duration of the speech periods. This in turn is fed into a pen-oscillograph. The pen recorder is set so as to make pauses apparent down to a length of one-tenth of a second—which is more than sufficiently accurate for showing up pauses relevant to output of words. Measurements were taken to an accuracy of one-tenth of a second (see Appendix II).

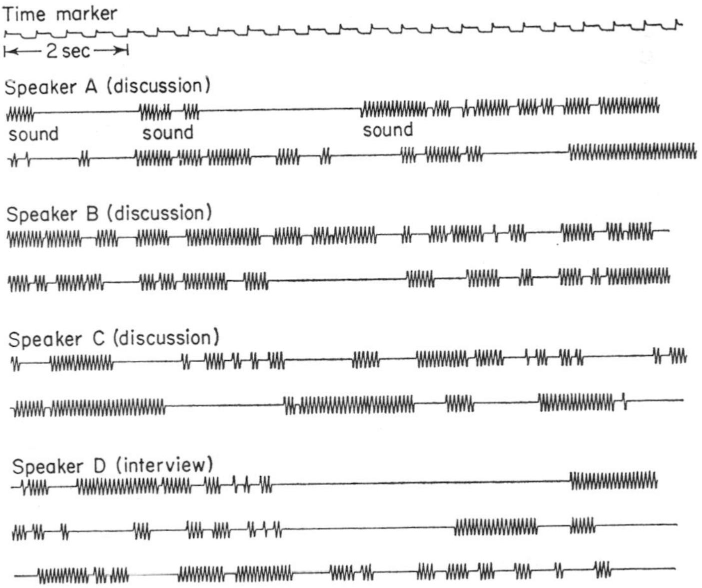

Time marker

|←— 2 sec —→|

Speaker A (discussion)

sound   sound   sound

Speaker B (discussion)

Speaker C (discussion)

Speaker D (interview)

FIG. 1 Graphic transformations of spontaneous speech by four speakers. Each line represents a period of 10 sec.

11

Figure 1 shows representations of such records of spontaneous speech by different speakers, in different situations, involving cognitive and emotional processes of various levels. The inspection of these records suffices to show that whatever these variations, continuity of sound production is not a characteristic of the act of generating spontaneous speech. What springs to notice immediately on seeing the visual transpositions of spoken language is the discontinuous nature of speech. We are not here concerned with the visual representation of speech sounds, the sonagrams as obtained from the speech spectrograph which give an acoustical description and a quasi-natural representation of the articulatory process of the production of speech, but we are interested in whether or not the articulatory process has taken place at all or whether there was inactivity of the articulatory muscles and therefore silence. Our record is one of presence or absence of sound produced in the course of connected speech, for it is not a record of sounds we wish to study, but the flow of natural speech as an indicator of the speaker's generative activity. Continuity in this context is judged by a different criterion than phonetic continuity. Altogether we may consider three types of gaps at which articulatory movement comes to a halt. There is (1) the discontinuity of phonation which occurs in articulatory shifts, e.g. when two plosives or stops follow each other (e.g. top part, tat tat). In such a case the breath stress is completely stopped and then released anew. (2) There is the discontinuity of phonation which is unrelated to any requirements of the articulatory processes themselves and is due to hesitation, and (3) there is the gap in speech when the phase of expiration comes to an end and a new supply of air is inhaled.

The first phonetic stoppage is part of articulation itself and the gaps in phonation are determined by the need to adjust the position of articulation. To be quite certain that no such gaps are included in our record, breaks in phonation of less than 0·25 sec were not considered as discontinuities. This might mean loss of some data, but it ensures the clear separation of hesitation pauses from phonetic stoppages.

Starting with this length as a minimum, extensive samples of speech derived from a variety of situations were analysed to answer the following questions:

(a) Where, within utterances, do pauses occur?
(b) What is the range and distribution of pause durations?
(c) How frequently do pauses occur, and what are the limits of continuity in speech sequences?

(a) The Placing of Hesitation Pauses

Speaking is, normally, a co-operative activity. Listeners co-operate with speakers by concentrating on the message; to comprehend it they must keep track of the context and integrate the elements of the message into the totality and structure of meaning, and this entails on the receptive side bridging the gaps that divide the elements of speech. Speakers co-operate with listeners by presenting their message in a form made to ease the listener's task of decoding. Ideally the act of speaking serves the communication of meaning. This is achieved best if the gaps introduced into the stream of speech are coincident with semantic groupings. Ideally then pauses should be found between phrases, at the joint points between clauses or at the end of sentences; in short they should be semantically determined and occur at grammatical junctures. When analysing our data, the following gaps in the flow of speech (pauses) were designated as grammatical junctures:

(1) "Natural" punctuation points, e.g. the end of a sentence.
(2) Immediately preceding a conjunction whether (i) co-ordinating, e.g. and, but, neither, therefore, or (ii) subordinating, e.g. if, when, while, as, because.
(3) Before relative and interrogative pronouns, e.g. who, which, what, why, whose.
(4) When a question is indirect or implied, e.g. "I don't know whether I will".
(5) Before all adverbial clauses of time (when), manner (how) and place (where).
(6) When complete parenthetical references are made, e.g. "You can tell that the words—this is the phonetician speaking—the words are not sincere".

Those gaps which occurred but were not covered by the rules given above we shall call non-grammatical. The following are examples of the most commonly occurring types of non-grammatical breaks:

(1) Where a gap occurs in the middle or at the end of a phrase, e.g. "In each of // the cells of the body // . . ."
(2) Where a gap occurs between words and phrases repeated, e.g. (i) "The question of the // of the economy". (ii) "This attitude is narrower than that // than that of many South Africans".
(3) Where a gap occurs in the middle of a verbal compound, e.g. "We have // taken issue with them and they are // resolved to oppose us".
(4) Where the structure of a sentence was disrupted by a reconsideration or a false start, e.g. "I think the problem of de Gaulle is the // what we have to remember about France is . . ."

When the placement of pauses according to these categories was examined comparing spontaneous speech with the reading of prepared texts (Goldman-Eisler, 1958, Henderson *et al.*, 1966) the phrasing of these texts, i.e. the grouping of the words by intermittent pauses, was almost entirely in terms of the sentence and clause structure of the passages investigated, i.e. following the rules of grammar. In the spontaneous speech examined (Henderson *et al.*, 1966) only 55% of pauses also occurred at grammatical junctures, while 45% of all pauses occurred in non-grammatical places. The explanation that pausing in spontaneous speech, as distinct from the reading of prepared texts, is by no means entirely controlled by grammatical structure will be sought further on. What seems clear is that a large proportion of pauses in spontaneous speech does not fit in with the linguistic structure and does not seem to serve communication, indeed it may at times impede rather than facilitate decoding.

(b) Length of Pauses

The duration of hesitation pauses in spontaneous speech presents us with an equally irrational picture if pauses are viewed as gaps instrumental in the grouping of meaningful phrases.

TABLE 1

Speech situations	Less than 0·5 sec	1·0 sec	2·0 sec	3·0 sec	3·0– 8·0 sec	8·0 sec and over
Percentage occurrence (means) of pauses of different duration						
Cartoon descriptions (spontaneous)	47·8	23·7	17·2	6·0	4·6	0·7
Cartoon interpretations (spontaneous)	43·6	19·8	16·3	8·8	9·6	1·9
Cartoon descriptions (learned)	59·6	24·3	12·7	2·7	0·7	0·0
Cartoon interpretations (learned)	63·7	20·0	13·5	2·0	0·8	0·0
Discussions (adults)	49·9	37·1	12·0	1·0	0·0	0·0
Discussions (adolescents)	41·4	41·1	16·0	1·3	0·1	0·0
Psychiatric interviews	16·4	33·9	28·6	10·8	9·6	0·6

Table 1 shows the distributions of pause durations for different samples of spontaneous speech (Goldman-Eisler, 1961c).

These pause measurements were based on speech of various kinds, in psychiatric interviews, in discussions with both adults and adolescents, in descriptions of cartoon serials (Fig. 11, pp. 51–52) and in the interpretations of their meaning. Measurements were also obtained from the latter two situations after they had been repeated six times, i.e. when they were well-learned and had lost their spontaneity.

The facts which emerged show that pausing during the act of generating spontaneous speech is a highly variable phenomenon which is symptomatic of individual differences, sensitive to the pressure of social interaction and to the requirements of verbal tasks and diminishing with learning, i.e. with the reduction in the spontaneity of the process.

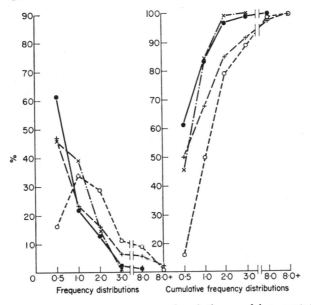

FIG. 2 Duration of pauses +————— + =descriptions and interpretations (spontaneous); •————————• =descriptions and interpretations (learned); ×————·———— × =discussions (adults and adolescents); ο—————————ο =interviews.

In more specific terms the findings were:

(1) that the lengths of individual pauses were distributed differently for different individuals,

(2) that the distribution of pause lengths was determined by the type of situation in which speech is uttered,

(3) that pauses in discussions were never longer than 3 sec and 99% were less than 2 sec and

(4) that familiarity with verbal material resulted in a reduction in time and frequency of pausing.

(c) The Frequency of Hesitation Pauses

The third question concerns the frequency with which pauses interrupt the even flow of speech. Somehow the phenomenon of speech has become associated with images which suggest continuity in sound production. We speak of the even flow, of fluency in speech, of a flood of language and many words relating to speech derive from descriptions of water in motion, such as "gush, spout, stream, torrent of speech, floodgates of speech", etc.

TABLE 2

Phrase length, i.e. number of words per pause (W/P): means for individuals

Situation: Cartoon experiment

Verbal Task:	Describing cartoons		Interpreting meaning	
	1st time	*7th time*	*1st time*	*7th time*
Subjects	W/P	W/P	W/P	W/P
Tho	6·0	8·8	4·6	4·0
Ha	4·4	7·2	3·6	6·1
Tr	4·3	5·4	3·8	4·9
Wi	3·7	8·3	3·9	10·9
Sa	4·6	5·3	5·5	6·5
Gi	5·6	6·0	5·6	4·2
Ne	5·5	7·0	5·7	5·7
Aa	3·2	3·7	2·5	3·3
Do	4·7	7·1	5·2	5·9

Situation: Discussion

Verbal Task: Debating

Subjects:	(1) Adult academic workers	(2) Adolescents	
	W/P	W/P	
A	5·3	11·7	6·3
B	11·1	9·3	7·2
C	12·9	4·3	2·8
C	5·8	8·0	11·1
D	11·1	5·6	8·7
		5·6	8·2
		8·0	7·2
		6·8	8·2

Situation: Psychiatric interview

Verbal Task: Relating personal history and background of illness

Subjects:	Neurotics
	W/P
M	5·3
B	6·3
S	6·3
H	6·4
P	5·2

The facts, however, show these images to be illusory; if we measure vocal continuity by the number of words uttered between two pauses, and call "phrase" the sequence uttered without break, we obtain a picture of fragmentation rather than of continuity. Table 2 (Goldman-Eisler 1961b) shows the mean phrase lengths for different subjects measured in number of words in different speech situations. Two factors appear to have a systematic effect on phrase length:

(1) individual differences which were highly significant, and
(2) differences in the conditions of speech production, e.g. between spontaneous utterance which is coincident with verbal planning, and the utterance of familiar sequences, well-learned after several repetitions.

Well-learned sequences have greater continuity and repetition leads to a closure of gaps. Figure 3 shows the cumulative percentage distribution of the mean phrase lengths in five speech situations. It shows that

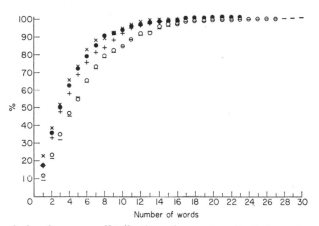

FIG. 3 Cumulative frequency distributions (percentages) of phrase lengths in five speech situations. ● = Descriptions (spontaneous); × = interpretations (spontaneous); ○ = descriptions (learned); + = interpretations (learned); — = psychiatric interviews.

in the situation in which speech was most unprepared and speakers least under social pressure, namely when describing or interpreting cartoons, 50% of speech is broken up into phrases of less than three words, 75% into phrases of less than five words, 80% into less than six words, 90% less than ten words, and that phrases of more than ten words uttered with fluency constitute only 10% of speech when speakers are describing pictures for the first time.

After having repeated their performance six times, only 35% of speech is broken into phrases of less than three words, while 50% are less than five words in length, 65% less than six words, 85% less than ten words and 90% less than twelve words. However, even in speech as well-learned as this, phrases with more than ten words are uttered only in 15% of cases.

The discontinuity of speech evident in the visual records analysed above (Fig. 1) is amply substantiated by these figures showing that at its most fluent, two-thirds of spoken language comes in chunks of less than six words.

(d) The Relative Duration of Pauses in Speech

Since spoken language is so fragmented and the flow of sound so frequently interrupted by non-phonetic hesitations, what proportion of utterance time is in fact filled with sound or taken up by silence? Interviews of eight subjects lasting thirty minutes to an hour showed that the mean proportions of utterance time taken up by pauses ranged between 4% and 54%. Even the more fluent speakers among these subjects (whose pause time proportion was less than 30%) produced on occasion utterances in which time was more than equally balanced between pausing and speaking (Goldman-Eisler, 1956c).

Discussions on various selected subjects showed a similar spread between 13% and 63% and impromptu talks on selected topics produced pause time proportions of between 35% and 67%.

A similar picture was obtained from spontaneous speech uttered in response to a request to describe picture stories (Goldman-Eisler, 1961). Again we have a wide variation from 16% to 62% of utterance time spent in silence. Most of the group, however, paused between 40% and 50% of their total speaking time. These values seem to be ample evidence that pausing is as much part of speech as vocal utterance.

(e) Pausing and the Rate of Speech Production

The rate of speech production expressed by the number of speech units, usually words or syllables, per total time of utterance is frequently used as a variable supposed to measure the speed of talking and as such brought in relation to other variables. It is therefore important that it is understood which aspect of speech production is in fact measured by speech rate, and what are its characteristic properties.

The following questions were asked (Goldman-Eisler, 1954) which preceded and stimulated the study of pausing:

(1) How does the speed of talking of one individual vary within a single conversation for the many separate utterances which he makes in the course of it?

(2) Does speed of talking discriminate between individuals, and what is their variability from conversation to conversation?

(3) What is the relation of speed of utterance to length of utterance?

Utterance here refers to a period of speech sandwiched between the last word of the interlocutor's preceding utterance and the first word of his following one.

Speed of talking (speech rate) was measured as the number of syllables per minute. The frequency distributions of speech rates show that there is a high degree of variability in the rate of speech production. Central tendencies, however, are very stable and individual differ-

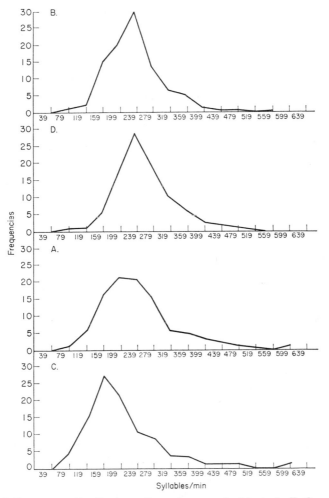

FIG. 4 Frequency distributions of speech rates of subjects A, B, C and D.

ences proved highly significant (see Table 3). For any given individual the rate of speech fluctuated at varying degrees in the different situations (see Table 4) but within the intra-individual range no systematic effect on speech rate was exercised by persons, the interlocutor emerging rather as one of the factors affecting the speed of talking.

The length of utterance, on the other hand, proved a major factor in the variability of the speech rate. This is illustrated in the scatter diagrams in Fig. 5 showing the relation between speed and the length of utterances for each of the subjects (A, B, C, D) based on all their utterances in the various conversations.

TABLE 3

Means and standard deviations of speech rates (number of syllables per minute) for subjects A, B, C, D (normals) and L, M, N, O (patients)

	Mean*	No. of syllables	S.D.	P		Mean	No. of syllables	S.D.	P
D	282·7	374	84·3		M	253·5	77	80·0	
B	257·1	274	77·0	0·001	O	245·9	104	68·6	0·001
A	247·3	295	86·8		L	222·1	104	70·5	
C	208·3	357	56·2		N	214·8	78	88·9	

* The means for *A, B, C, D* are based on readings from all their conversations.

TABLE 4

Results of analysis of variance testing the differences in speech rates in different conversational situations for subjects A, B, C, D

Subject	Conversation	Means	S.D.	F ratio	P
A	With B	216·7	57·5		
	With C	254·5	58·3		
	With D	206·0	80·4	4·8	0·01
	With B, C	209·5	23·2		
	With B, C, D	244·8	24·4		
B	With A	206·1	31·3		
	With C	193·8	36·5		
	With D	252·2	56·9	16·3	0·001
	With A, C	237·2	52·5		
	With A, C, D	275·7	42·9		
C	With A	181·0	46·1		
	With B	186·6	29·1		
	With D	187·5	48·5	1·5	N.S.
	With A, B	206·2	96·4		
	With A, B, D	214·5	39·6		
D	With A	244·8	52·1		
	With B	273·0	44·3	3·18	0·05
	With C	272·7	87·3		
	With A, B, C	274·1	41·3		

It is evident from this that the speech rates lying along the base of the distribution are derived entirely from short utterances rarely containing more than 40 syllables, while the centre of the distribution includes all the long utterances. The length of utterances thus impinges upon their

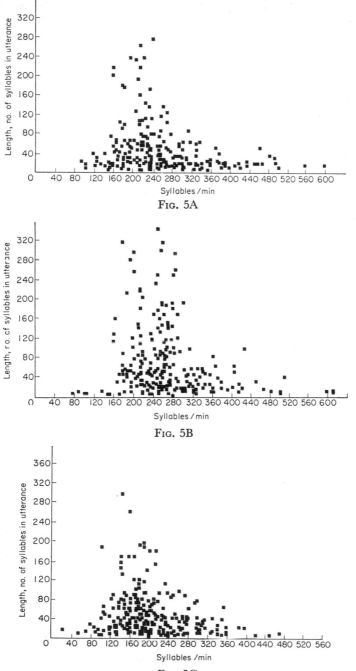

FIG. 5A

FIG. 5B

FIG. 5C

speech rates in the following ways: (a) the range of speech rates is relatively great for short utterances, but narrows as utterances grow longer, (b) stability is gained at a length of about 100 syllables. Speech

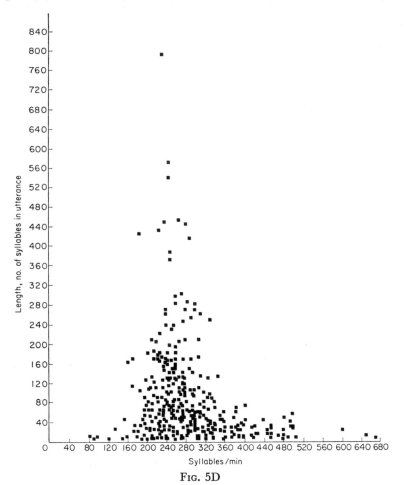

Fɪɢ. 5D

Fɪɢ. 5 Scatter diagram showing relation of speed and length of utterances for subjects A, B, C and D.

rates for utterances longer than that are confined within a narrow range of central position, and (c) relatively fast speech rates occur rarely at lengths above 60 syllables per utterance and *never* above 100 syllables, and (d) means and standard deviations of speech rates for utterances of different lengths decreased with the increasing length of utterance (see Table 5): the stabilization of speed in talking gaining stability as it slows down.

In spite of the wide scatter, speech rates for short utterances as well as long ones discriminated between individuals with high significance.

The fact that on no occasion were longer utterances spoken at high speeds suggested that a physical as well as a psychological factor might be operating as an impediment; the high rates of speech output sometimes achieved in bursts seemed on this basis physically impossible to maintain for any length of time. Short utterances were not necessarily always faster than long ones, in the case of the former the range of speed was wider from very slow (60 syllables per min) to very fast (600 syllables per min). What discriminated the short from the long utterances, then, was not only the rates at which they were spoken, but the inherent difference in the amount of freedom to vary the rate of speech.

TABLE 5

Means and standard deviations of rates of talking for different lengths of utterances based on all speech samples recorded of A, B, C, D, and on interview recorded of L, M, N, O

Length of utterance	A, B, C, D			L, M, N, O		
	No. of utterances	Mean	S.D.	No. of utterances	Mean	S.D.
5–19	319	272·3	108·0	109	264·6	99·7
20–39	315	254·2	79·7	85	244·4	53·9
40–59	218	239·2	71·2	46	219·1	45·6
60–79	119	233·2	56·4⎤	50	207·9	31·3
80–99	84	237·6	53·9⎦			
100–199*	165	230·8	40·8⎤	73	206·5	30·0
200 and over	78	229·8	31·0⎦			

* Owing to the decrease in the frequency of utterances with increase in length, the speech rates underlying the means of utterances longer than 100 syllables were grouped into larger intervals.

Two kinds of delay suggested themselves as factors responsible for the variations in speech rate: delays due to the planning and organizing of utterances and delays due to breath intakes during speech.

The original assumption (Goldman-Eisler, 1954) viewed both interruptions in the flow of vocal sound as of about equal weight in contributing to the delay. Measurements of the relative time taken up in hesitation and spent in inhaling air showed however, that the principal factor in holding up the smooth flow of vocal production in speech was pausing in hesitation, rather than that due to the biological necessity of drawing air into the lungs. Breath pauses range according to our measurements between half a second and a second, with some breath pauses in very fast speech being as short as a quarter second. Measurements of breath rates during speech (Goldman-Eisler, 1955, 1956b) revealed for the most part a range between 2 and 20 respirations a minute.

Thus breathing might normally occupy between 1·5 and 15 seconds in a minute, i.e. between 2·5 and 25 % of the total speaking time. Measurements of periods of hesitation based on the same samples on the other hand showed these to occupy an average of between 40 and 50 % of the total speaking time of one person (see page 18).

It seemed from these figures that the fluctuations in speech rate must be a function of the duration and the frequency of hesitation pauses to a much greater extent than of breathing pauses. This posed the questions: (a) of the extent to which the amount of pausing in the flow of speech determined speech rate and its fluctuations, (b) of what the determining influence was of the absolute speed of talking, i.e. the speed of actual articulation upon the overall rate of speech, or total speech rate and finally (c) what were the internal relations of total or overall speech rate, articulation rate and the length of hesitation pauses in speech, if speech rate (SR) is measured as the number of syllables a minute of the whole utterance, articulation rate (AR) as the number of syllables a minute of the time spent in vocal activity, and length of hesitation pauses as the proportion of time spent in silence (PP).

Table 6 (Goldman-Eisler, 1956) lists the mean and standard deviations of SR, PP and AR, and it may be seen from it that there is a close inverse relation between the proportional duration of hesitation pauses (PP) in speech utterances and the speech rate (SR). The longer and more frequent the pauses, the slower is the total rate of speech production. The rank correlation coefficient was $-0·940$. The articulation rate (AR) on the other hand, plays no significant part in the rate at which speech is produced over a period of time (SR) (rank coefficient $r_{SR/AR} = -0·173$). A similar absence of relationship ($0·207$—insignificant) between absolute speaking and total time of utterance was found by Henze (1953), whilst total time of utterance was correlated ($0·730$) with the time taken up by pauses. This seems not surprising if we compare the variability of the articulation rate (variation coefficient $=9·1$ %) with that of the pauses (variation coefficient $=45·9$ %). The variation coefficient for SR was $21·5$ %.

The range of pause time in relation to speech was therefore, in this sample, five times that of the rate of articulation. The actual rate of articulation occupied a range between 4·4 and 5·9 syllables per second. In individuals this range reduces to a characteristic discriminating between individuals at a high level of significance (P less than $0·001$).

Phoneticians have investigated the limits in speed of articulation and have found it to vary between 6·7 and 8·2 syllables per second according to articulator (Miller, 1951). These investigations were carried out by asking subjects to repeat (as fast as they could) simple syllables in rhythmic groups. Thus tat, tat, tat was used to measure the speed of articulatory movements made with the tip of the tongue which produced 8·2 syllables per second, whereas only 6·7 syllables can be produced with the back of the tongue.

Our measurements given above are based on normally structured speech uttered spontaneously in the context of the interview situation. While being slower, as one might expect in the more leisurely interview situation, the range covered of 4·4 to 5·9 syllables is equally narrow.

TABLE 6

Means (M), standard deviations (s.d.), and variation coefficients (s.d./$M \times 100$) or V of speech rates (SR), percentage time of pauses (PP), and articulation rates (AR), for utterances from interviews with eight subjects

	SR			PP			AR			Number of utterances
	M	s.d.	V	M	s.d.	V	M	s.d.	V	
S. I.	4·3	0·78	18·1	4·4	4·01	91·1	4·5	0·75	16·6	26
Co.	3·9	0·53	13·6	19·3	10·4	53·8	4·9	1·12	22·8	53
He.	3·7	0·44	11·8	27·9	18·2	65·2	5·0	1·03	20·6	11
S. I. I.	3·3	1·09	35·8	29·8	9·7	32·5	4·7	0·54	11·5	15
Jo.	3·3	0·93	28·2	34·3	12·5	36·4	5·0	0·69	13·3	29
Mu.	2·8	0·78	27·8	43·6	12·9	29·6	5·2	1·06	20·4	54
Pea.	2·7	0·45	16·6	53·2	15·0	28·2	5·9	1·48	25·1	46
B. I.	2·3	0·81	35·2	47·6	14·3	30·0	4·4	0·60	13·7	33

Standard deviations (s.d.) and coefficients of variations (V) of means for eight subjects

SR		PP		AR	
s.d.	V	s.d.	V	s.d.	V
0·71	21·5%	14·92	45·9%	0·45	9·1%

Rates of articulation based on three conditions of speech production (a) the description of cartoon stories, (b) the interpretation of their meaning, and (c) speech uttered after several repetitions, when descriptions and interpretations were well-practised, were calculated (Goldman-Eisler, 1961b) in terms of words per second. There were some highly significant individual differences ($p < 0.001$) but no difference was found between the two highly distinct cognitive operations of describing and interpreting picture stories (in both situations AR was 3·7 words per second) indicating that the rate of articulation is a personality constant of remarkable invariance. This invariance, however, proved subject to modification as a result of practice. Comparing the speech before and after practice (six repetitions of original spontaneous text), the descriptions showed an increase of 3·5 to 4·0 words per second and the interpretations an increase from 3·6 to 4·1 words per second. The difference was significant at the 0·01 level of probability.

B

This difference in the response of AR to changes in the levels of verbal planning and to practice seems to lend support to the idea that the difference between spontaneity and practice is more basic than between two different levels of cognitive complexity in verbal planning. Such a basic division as the former is, of course, contained in the old-established duality formulated by Hughlings Jackson as voluntary or propositional versus automatic and well-organized speech. AR thus becomes an efficient and unequivocal indicator of habit strength only. It is closely allied to the peripheral act of phonation reflecting its smoothness of operation, whilst being independent of the central act of propositionizing (i.e. of constructing propositions).

Considering that the mechanics of speech production are in the normal adult a skill of high order and stability of output is characteristic of skilful performances, the relative invariance of the rate of articulation is not surprising.

What seemed to be a variation in the speed of talking thus turned out to be variation in amount of pausing. As in the analysis of the visual records of speech, the illusory nature of our experience of speed in talking as a matter of speech movements is again revealed.

What is experienced as increase of speed in talking is therefore due largely to the closing of gaps and to the heightened continuity with which movements performed at a relatively constant rate succeed each other. Naturally with speech which is little interrupted by pauses, the speed of talking becomes a function of the rate of articulation or speed of speech movements themselves. But such uninterrupted flow proved, with adults at least, a rare phenomenon when speech is spontaneous and unprepared.

(f) Pauses and the Generative Processes in Speech

The variability of pause length as well as pause frequency and occurrence under different conditions of speech production and with different individuals raises it to an extremely significant aspect of speech behaviour. It is important to understand its function if we wish to understand the process of speech production generally. If the relative invariance of the rate of articulation was the result of the speech movements having reached a high level of skill, one might suppose that pauses represent that aspect of the speech act which has little call on skill and which reflects the non-skill part of the speech process. One might therefore regard pausing as an attribute of spontaneity in the creation of new verbal constructions and structures, i.e. of verbal planning. Continuous and rapid vocalization on the other hand would be the result of practice and thus occur in the use of well-learned word sequences. In this respect speech would be no different from any other activity which is subject to learning. This assumption was amply confirmed by measurements of speech produced in conditions of great spontaneity as compared with well-learned speech (see Fig. 6) (Goldman-Eisler 1961a).

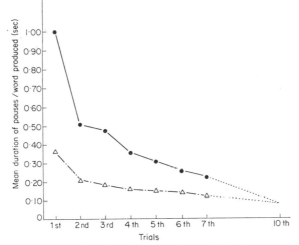

FIG. 6 Hesitancy at two levels of verbal planning and its decrease with repetition. △ = Descriptions, • = interpretation.

(g) Pauses and the Duality of Language

The fact that delay is an integral part of the process of speech production, particularly when utterances are new and spontaneous, ties in with other facts which had emerged from the study of the speech of the brain damaged (Jackson, 1932). It is also relevant to the problem of the dual nature of speech mentioned before and the problem of the relation between speaking and thinking. The dual nature of speech and language has puzzled generations of thinkers and this is reflected in various conceptual systems, each emphasizing more or less different aspects of its dichotomy. Concerning the role of speech in relation to thinking, the neglect of the duality principle and the rigid, undynamic, all-or-nothing approach to this problem is responsible for much of the confusion which characterizes the unending controversy about the speech-thought relationship.

These controversies have thrown up roughly three groups: the proponents of the belief in the identity of thinking and the act of speaking, and those who believe in the primacy of thought to speech, taking up extremist positions, while the third group consists of those who consider that language functions in two ways; as an instrument in the thinking process, stimulating and aiding it, and as a substitute for thinking masking its absence or even inhibiting the thinking process. Activity would in this case be diverted from the central to more facile peripheral channels of automatic verbalization, and a kind of verbal bondage imposed.[1]

Healthy, normal speech would, according to the third group, represent the integration of these two processes which constantly alternate and interact with each other and are represented in different degrees.

It was Hughlings Jackson who first broke away from the monistic theory of language which had the support of scientific thinkers—the so-called interjectional theory. Since Democritus propounded the thesis that human speech originates in certain sounds of a merely emotional character, the idea that human speech can be reduced to outcries of fear, rage or joy, not specific to man, and that the social fact of speech can be traced back to this general biological cause, has had a profound appeal to men of science. The assumption that a direct path leads from interjection to speech gained further support through Darwin (1873) when he showed that expressive sounds or acts are dictated by certain biological needs and used according to definite biological rules. As a result of studying language disorders, Hughlings Jackson (1878) came to insist on a sharp distinction between interjectional or emotional language and what he called "propositional" speech. Jackson held that speech cannot be pieced together from words which precede it, but that on the contrary, words follow from speech as a whole. Single words, he maintained are meaningless and so is any unrelated succession of words. The unit of speech is a proposition. A single word is, or is in effect, a proposition, if other words in relation are implied. The exclamation "Fire!" is a proposition if it is intended to tell passers-by that a fire has broken out. The words "yes" and "no" are propositions, if used for assent and dissent. According to Jackson, all the truly intellectual power of language, everything that it accomplishes for thought, is contained in this power of "statement", of predication.

In contrast to speech of this kind, to "superior" speech, he designates speech in which words have only the interjectional or emotional use, but not the prepositional, as "inferior" speech. This includes ready-made phrases or clichés, i.e. "old" speech, e.g. "very well" or "I don't think so", of which emotional interjections and ejaculations are a subclass. The nervous arrangements for such "automatic" speech he assumed to be well-organized. By "superior" speech he referred to speech that is new, though not necessarily composed of new words nor new combinations of words; it consists of propositions symbolizing relations of images new to the speaker, as e.g. when a speaker carefully describes something novel; he called generating speech of this kind "propositionizing".

Hughlings Jackson considered this difference as the most significant criterion for classifying speech phenomena. It is the difference between subconscious and automatic processes on the one hand and conscious and voluntary processes on the other. Both involve the service of words. Hughlings Jackson associated the unconscious and automatic service of words with the right half of the brain, and the conscious and voluntary service of words in speech with the left half.[2]

At the same time Jackson maintains that in healthy speech the two processes function in duplicate. The thing which is important to show says Jackson, is that "mentation" is dual and that physically the unit of function of the nervous system is double the unit of composition; not that one-half of the brain is "automatic" and the other "voluntary". The more automatic the process is, or becomes by repetition, the more equally and fully it is represented doubly in each half of the brain.

As mentioned before (p. 9), Jackson's discrimination between the two types of speech was dynamic, introducing the element of time and stipulating circumstance as a criterion for the classification of speech as "superior" or "inferior", "voluntary" or "automatic", "propositional" or "emotional". Jackson postulates the mental corollary of "clear pre-conception" as the necessary element to distinguish voluntary from "automatic" utterances.

"In voluntary speech the prior reproduction of words constitutes the preconception. If a man utters, as applying to a new set of circum-stances, the most automatic utterance he has, if he utters anything 'for the sake of uttering it' as when asked to do so, there is then a voluntary utterance, for then the operation occurs after clear preconception."

Disease demonstrates that this distinction is not a fanciful one. With speechless patients the "same" is never the same. He may be unable to "say", i.e. to utter for the sake of uttering it (a voluntary act), what he has just uttered as part of an involuntary process.

The difference is that in the one case the utterance is the result of an act of decision, while in the case of the involuntary, automatic utterance we deal with verbal sequences which through practice have become verbal habits associated with a particular concrete situation. It is in this sense "organized", a part of a whole situation complex and linked to it by association or conditioning.

I have presented the gist of Jackson's ideas and conclusions at some length because the subsequent divisions which are relevant to our problem originate from it.

Henry Head (1926) changed Jackson's designation of the "proposi-tional" use of words, and spoke of symbolic expression and symbolic formulation, while not limiting this symbolic function to language alone. While this is a significant step beyond Jackson, Head maintained the dichotomy between the "superior", "voluntary", "symbolic" stratum and inferior, direct (i.e. mechanically released or automatic) and non-symbolic acts.

Goldstein (1948) moved from Jackson's neurological viewpoint to the standpoint of behaviour, i.e. of the organism acting in relation to its environment as part of a whole situation complex. He makes a sharp distinction between the immediate and the mediated and the presentative and the representative content, when referring to the content of perceptive experiences; between the direct "data" of these experiences and the representative function they fulfil. He distinguishes two different kinds of attitude—concrete and abstract; "We act concretely when we enter a room in darkness and push the button for light. If, however, we desist from pushing the button, reflecting that by pushing the button we might awaken someone asleep in the room, then we are acting abstractly. We transcend the immediate given specific aspect of sense impression, we detach ourselves from the latter and consider the situation from a conceptual point of view, and react accordingly. This again is voluntary action and implies inhibition. By inhibiting an impulse we divide ourselves in two" (Goldstein, 1948).

These attitudes of action and reflection appear also in language and concrete language is the use of the ". . . instrumentalities of speech, the automatic use of sounds, series of words, sentences, etc., of language in familiar situations and emotional language; abstract language on the other hand is volitional, propositional and rational" (Goldstein, 1948).

That pausing in speech utterances is relevant in this context seems a reasonable proposition. We need only to consider the close relationship between the phenomena of thought (whether we refer to symbolic processes or to the volitional acts of choice) and of delay of action. The relationship between the latter and the number of alternatives from which choice is to be made (Garner, 1962) and the dependence of delayed reactions on the preconditions for the functioning of symbolic processes are well established facts (Mowrer, 1960). Thus the capacity to hold a response "in suspension" for a delay period varies with the phylogenetic level of the organism and the length of the delay period increases as one ascends the evolutionary scale and with the progressive elaboration of the frontal lobes. Surgical assault upon the frontal lobes typically impairs this capacity. Capacity for delay and capacity for symbolic representation are consequently functions of the same developmental levels and neurological substrata. If the silences which interrupt the vocal activity of speech are considered to be hesitations delaying subsequent utterance, the hypothesis that they mask and are concomitant with symbolic processes which are active in the speaker is a reasonable deduction. The experiments designed to test this hypothesis are described in the following chapters.

Summary to Chapter 1

We have listed in this chapter some facts concerning five aspects of the behaviour of hesitation pauses in spontaneous speech and tried to deduce with their help hypotheses as to what their function might be in the process of generating spontaneous speech. These were:

(1) The placing of hesitation pauses. Spontaneous speech was found to differ from readings of prepared texts in that a large proportion of pauses in spontaneous speech does not fit in with the linguistic structure, and does not serve communication.

(2) The duration of hesitation pauses was shown to be a highly variable phenomenon, symptomatic of individual differences, sensitive to the pressures of social interaction and to the requirements of verbal tasks and diminishing with learning, i.e. with the reduction in the spontaneity of the process.

(3) Spontaneous speech was shown to be a highly fragmented and discontinuous activity. When even at its most fluent, two-thirds of spoken language comes in chunks of less than six words, the attribute of flow and fluency in spontaneous speech must be judged an illusion.

(4) The actual proportion of pausing time in utterances, while subject to considerable variation, was high enough to justify the conclusion that pausing is as much part of speech as vocal utterance.

(5) Consistent with this the rate of speech production turned out to be a function of the proportion of time taken up by hesitation pauses. Variations in the overall speed of talking were found to be variations in the amount of pausing. What is experienced as increase of speed in talking proved to be variation in amount of pausing. The rate of articulation based on vocal activity exclusively, on the other hand, was shown to be relatively invariant.

This difference in variability between the rate of speech movements and the amount of pausing was interpreted as a reflection of the difference between the skill and non-skill parts of the speech process. Pausing was as a consequence assumed to be an attribute of spontaneity in the creation of new verbal constructions, i.e. of verbal planning, masking and being concomitant with the cognitive processes which are active in speakers who think "on their feet".

Chapter 2

The Significance of Hesitation Pauses

Experiments

In the experiments to be described below hesitation pauses were treated as one manifestation of the more general blocking of activity which occurs when organisms are confronted with situations of uncertainty, and when the selection of the next step requires an act of choice.

A speaker engaged in spontaneous speech is required to keep making three kinds of decision as he proceeds in the production of speech:

(1) The first type is a content decision, which narrows the field of linguistic activity in terms of "what" he wants to say. One must imagine that some of this content is tied to key words, that frequently the semantic choice is inseparable from the lexical, but that these key words stand out as semantic landmarks mapping the area of discourse, and at this stage exist as yet in isolation, independent of sequential ties. Other content must be imagined unverbalized and still in need and search of its linguistic incarnation.

(2) Before a person can begin to utter coherent language, however, he must have ready at least the broad outline of a syntactic structure. This requires decisions of a syntactic nature.

(3) The third set of choices concerns itself with the selection of words to fit the syntactic framework in accordance with the semantic plan. Some follow from the context or grammar, others need to be fitted to a specific meaning intended to be conveyed. Here the referential aspect is more important for word choice than the sequential ties; the scope of possible choices is wider and the uncertainty greater.

All three kinds of decision were expected to result in a delay of the external speech act. This implies that verbal planning and its vocal execution—or as some writers (Vygotsky, 1962, Kainz, 1954) prefer to refer to the division, internal and external speech—must alternate. Central and peripheral linguistic processes would be successive links in the verbal sequence where this requires central processing. This is in conformity with the law of the unity of attention which was found to be particularly effective in acts of low probability (Broadbent, 1958), i.e. when choice is made among many alternatives.

Our contention therefore was that decisions of a lexical and structural kind as well as of content made in the course of speech utterances must be accompanied by an arrest of the speech act, i.e. by pausing.

The problem was how to test these propositions in respect of each of the three types of choice, i.e. how to adjudicate the event to their separate occurrence.

(a) Incidence of Pauses and Lexical Decisions

Let us take the hypothesis concerning the lexical choice of words, namely that hesitation pauses in speech represent the act of choice in selecting the suitable word from among the possible alternative words. To test this we must have an experimental situation which discriminates, as far as possible, between such pauses as may be related to decisions of content or sentence structure. This is done when the study is confined to those hesitation pauses which only occur within sentences. We assume that once a speaker has uttered the first word of a sentence, he is on his course; he has decided not only what to say but has created for himself at least the broad syntactical framework. The pauses, except those occurring at clause junctures, can now be stipulated to be lexical ones. The hypothesis concerning these was formulated in the following terms.

HYPOTHESIS

If language is viewed as a series of events structured in sequences of words, the context in which these occur will have a limiting or constraining effect on the speaker's choice of words.

In statistical terms this hypothesis is implied when speech is said to be a Markoff process. Each successive symbol is chosen according to the transition probabilities which depend, at any stage, on preceding choices as well as on the particular symbols themselves. These symbols represent the influence of the probabilities of word occurrence and thus the frequency of use of symbols in the language at large, plus the constraints derived from the context and the structure of language. At such stages in the process where the probability of choice is less dependent on the previous choices, the speaker is said to have greater freedom of choice. It is reasonable to expect the hesitation pauses in speech to occur at these stages. Their function might be conceived of as serving the selection processes which direct the course of verbal sequences at points where constraints become weaker and choices more uncertain.

This set of circumstances is most fittingly formulated within the conceptual framework of information theory. Accordingly "greater freedom of choice" and "higher uncertainty" imply "a greater amount of information". Lounsbury (1954) formulated this hypothesis as follows: "Hesitation pauses correspond to the points of highest statistical uncertainty in the sequencing of units in any given order."

Words uttered after some hesitation may therefore be expected to show a decrease in transition probability and in that sense carry an increase in information.

EXPERIMENTAL PROCEDURE

To test this hypothesis the incidence of hesitation pauses in the utterance of sentences in spontaneous speech had to be related to the transition probabilities of the words constituting them. Our experiment was designed to yield estimates of transition probabilities to be related to the pauses which had been made when the sentences had originally been uttered.

The experimental procedure involved providing the subjects with the preceding context in the recorded conversation as far as it was relevant to the experimental sentence, and then asking them to guess the first and each successive word in the sentence, continuing to the last until the sentence was complete. Each subject was given one minute to guess each word. If in that period he failed to guess it, he was told the right word and asked to proceed to the next. At each stage he was handed a card with the text of the sentence up to and including the last word guessed. He thus made his guesses on the basis of the preceding context.

This is an adaptation of the technique which Shannon (1951) used in the prediction of printed English which was concerned with the guessing of letters. The guessing of words presents new problems. The range of possible word choices, for instance, is a manifold of the small number of possible letter choices, and at points of great uncertainty it often tends to be almost inexhaustible. In order to give the correct word a fair chance to appear among the alternatives guessed, several samples had to be picked from the store of language, that is, several subjects were used to predict each sentence.

In an attempt to see how many samples from the store of language are required to exhaust the supply of possible alternatives, the experiment—carried on for a full minute every time—was continued with one of the sentences until guesses from 15 subjects were obtained; in other words 15 samples have been taken from the store of possible alternatives in the language.

Figure 7 shows examples of cumulative curves for easily predictable words and words of poor predictability. In guessing the latter, each subject was able to add a new range of alternative guesses. The trend of the cumulative curve for these words shows that the alternatives suggested by 15 subjects are still far from exhausting the number of possible alternatives. In the case of the words which were easily predicted the number of alternative guesses decreased with each additional guesser and soon reached a plateau. Hardly more than 5 to 6 samples (i.e. guessers) were required to exhaust the number of possible alternatives provided by language, though there may have been some highly individual stragglers here and there. The results reported below are based

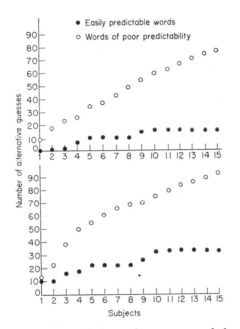

Fig. 7 Cumulative curves of alternative guesses made by 15 subjects.

on the guesses of 6 highly educated and linguistically sophisticated subjects. This number of samples was, judged by this experiment, sufficiently large for estimating the predictability of any word or its transition probability in the sequence used.

ESTIMATING TRANSITION PROBABILITIES

The transition probabilities were the ratios of the frequency of correct guesses to the total number of guesses made. If none of the guesses was correct, transition probability was taken to be zero. If there were no incorrect guesses, i.e. if the first guess was correct each time, it was estimated as 1·0. The failure of any of the subjects to guess correctly at the first attempt brought this estimate down accordingly.

MATERIAL

Twelve sentences of varying length, complexity and structure, coming from four speakers, were subjected to this procedure. They contained a total of 348 words, their length ranging between 16 and 51 words and they contained a total of 60 pauses. There was no relation between length of sentence and number of pauses per sentence. The difference in the levels of complexity of the sentences cut across the differences in length. Among the short as well as the long sentences were those with one or more dependent clauses inserted between subject and predicate, and those in which clauses were independent and cumulative (18 words to 45 words). Altogether they may be said to represent a fairly wide range of spontaneous language.

Three of these sentences were taken from a recorded debate on the best form of Government, two speakers contributing (one and two sentences, respectively). Five sentences came from an interview with a highly intelligent neurotic patient. Four sentences came from a letter which had been dictated especially for the experiment. The person who dictated it was unprepared as to what kind of letter was required of him. He was asked to start at once, not to prepare the letter in his mind, i.e. to speak spontaneously. The recording on tape started at once.

The criteria for the selection of sentences for the experiment from the recorded and transcribed speech were as follows:

(1) They should be grammatically correct and well constructed, and
(2) They should be logically consistent with the context of the whole utterance. This eliminated a large mass of recorded material of spontaneous speech.

Gaps in the output of sound not less than 0·25 sec were classified as hesitation pauses irrespective of their length. Although they were distributed over a wide range of durations (0·25 to 6·0 sec) they were treated as a category, because the problem at this stage was a generic one, concerned with the significance of the event of speech coming to a pause, irrespective of its extent in time.

EXPERIMENT 1

There were two series of experiments. In the first experiment the subjects were asked to guess by starting with the first word and continuing one by one to the last, following in the normal way the forward direction of language. Seven sentences containing 212 words and 34 pauses were predicted in this way.

The original data consisted of alternative words guessed by the subjects for each successive word in any sentence. The series either ended with the correct guess or, where there was no correct guess, included all the words suggested in the minute allowed for guessing. After the first set of word predictions of any sentence had been obtained, the guesses made by the succeeding subjects consisted of two kinds of words: unique guesses which were specific to a specific subject and words which were guessed by more than one subject. Only one occurrence of each word was included into the total number of all the different words suggested.

The transition probabilities estimated were as mentioned above; the ratios of frequency of correct guesses to the sum of different words suggested.

To test the hypothesis that hesitation pauses correspond to the points of highest statistical uncertainty in the sequencing of units in any given order, the distributions of these probabilities were compared for the following classes of words:

(1) The words which were uttered without hesitation which will be referred to as words uttered fluently or f.

(2) The words utterance of which was preceded by hesitation (they will be referred to as words following pauses or h).

The first group of words uttered fluently (f) contained 178 words, i.e. 84% of all words uttered in our sentences.

The second group, the words following pauses (h) contained 34 words or as many as there were pauses, i.e. 16% of all the words in our sentences. Twenty-eight out of these 34 words which followed pauses had transition probabilities not exceeding 0·10, while of the 34 words which preceded the pauses only five had transition probabilities of less than 0·10. Most pauses are thus followed by a decline of transition probability (or increase of information).

The relationship, however, was not reciprocal. Forty-six of the 75 words of low predictability ($p=0$ or 0·10) were not preceded by pauses but by fluent speech. According to this result, pauses in most cases preceded an increase of information but information was increased as frequently when it was not preceded by a pause.

EXPERIMENT 2

The purpose of the second experiment was to evaluate the above fact. The theoretical consideration which led to the new set of experiments was that forward dependencies between words were not likely to cover all the sequential dependencies which structure imposes upon language.

PROCEDURE

Six new sentences (containing 136 words and 26 pauses) were subjected not only to predictions in the forward direction from left to right, but also to predictions in reverse direction starting with the last word and working from right to left. As before, the previous text of the conversation, as far as it was relevant to the experimental sentence, was read to the subject. He was then asked to guess the sentence, starting with guesses for the last word and continuing, word by word, until he had reached the first. After guessing each word, whether with or without success (i.e. after one minute), he was handed a card containing the last word, the last but one, the last three words, etc., at each stage, respectively.

SUBJECTS

There were again altogether six subjects to guess each sentence. Three guessed from left to right and three from right to left. The subjects were equated as best as possible for intelligence and linguistic sophistication. Subjects whose proportions of correct guesses fell short of the standard set by the group were eliminated. Most of the subjects in these experiments were academic personnel.

RESULTS

(1) Right to left guessing, although subjectively felt by the guessers to be much more difficult, was objectively almost as successful as left to right guessing. Fifty-eight per cent of all words were, on the average, predicted with varying degrees of probability in forward guessing and 53% in reverse guessing. (This agrees fairly well with Shannon's (1951) 50% redundancy. The sentences used in these experiments may therefore be taken as fairly representative samples of language at large.)

Altogether 86% were predictable with some probability one way or the other, 14% remained quite unpredictable either way. Of these 14% most words were preceded by pauses.

(2) When the number of different alternatives for each word in the sentence as guessed in the left to right direction was plotted against the number of different alternatives suggested when the sentences were guessed going from right to left (see Fig. 8), it became clear that a good number of words which are of poor predictability when approached with the information of previous context become easily predictable when the guesser has information of what follows rather than what precedes in speech. In other words, the occurrence of some words is constrained by previous context and of others by subsequent context. Other words again were easily predicted whether approached from the beginning (left) or from the end (right) of the sentence, and a small number (23) proved extremely indeterminate, the frequency of wrong guesses being equally high in both directions.

Figure 8 shows these equidistant guesses enclosed within a least square space containing those words which had stimulated more than 10 guesses both ways. There were 23 of them and 17 belonged to words which in the original utterance had been preceded by pauses. The χ^2 based on this grouping was 56·8, the significance level far exceeding $p=0·001$.

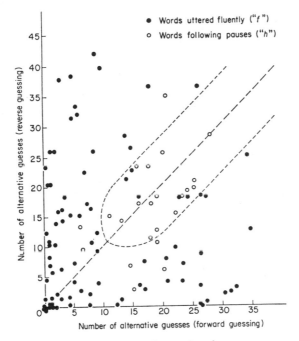

Fig. 8 Diagram showing relation between forward and reverse guesses and position of alternatives guessed in respect of least square space.

ESTIMATING TRANSITION PROBABILITIES

The transition probabilities were estimated as before, for left to right or right to left guesses separately, to be then combined and averaged. Figure 9 (A, B and C) shows the distributions for the three classes of words to be compared along the scale of transition probabilities as estimated on the basis of guessing the sentences in (A) the left to right direction, (B) right to left direction and of (C) combining and averaging these figures. Adding and averaging the expectancies due to constraint coming from the right and those due to forward constraint coming from the left reduced the extreme improbability as well as extreme probability of the words which had been uttered fluently. Their distribution, more or less U-shaped when based on forward or reverse guesses separately, becomes normalized and shows a regression towards the mean. Word utterance in fluent speech seems, according to this, to be subject to the laws of chance.

By contrast, the words the utterance of which was delayed, i.e. which followed the pauses, remained improbable, even when forward and backward probabilities were combined. They were consistently unpredictable, whichever way they were approached by the guesser, i.e.

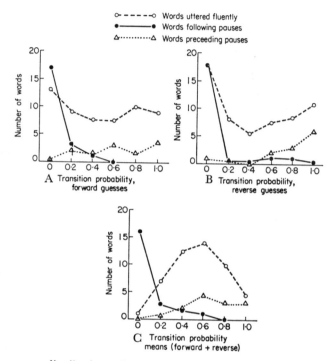

FIG. 9 Frequency distributions of transition probabilities for words uttered fluently, words following pauses and words preceding pauses based on forward guesses, reverse guesses and averaged forward and reverse guesses.

they showed themselves relatively independent of verbal context, preceding or subsequent. Averaging their transition probabilities produces no change in the shape of their distribution. Their occurrence must be regarded as a matter of choice rather than of chance.

A similar tendency at the opposite pole of the probability scale can be observed in the distributions of the words which preceded pauses. These tend to be consistently easily predictable whether approached from the left, the beginning, or from the right, the end, of sentences.

Analysing the same data in respect of word length, we find that the gradient from information to redundancy in word sequences between two pauses coincides with one from maximum to minimum length of word. The words which followed the pauses had a mean length of 7·1 letters per word. The mean length of words preceding pauses measured in letters was 2·7.

The line in Fig. 10 represents the mean letter length of the words in the different probability classes. Its extremes, which are also the extremes of transition probability, coincide with their position in the sentences in respect of pauses.

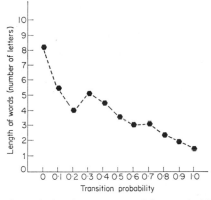

FIG. 10 Diagram showing relation between transition probabilities and letter length of words.

This again links up with the grammatical categories of the words preceding and following pauses, the latter tending to be not only long but also content words while most of the former were not only short but also structural words. These relationships in our data are in line with the known facts of language statistics (Herdan, 1960).

CONCLUSION AND DISCUSSION

As a result of the second set of experiments including reverse as well as forward predictions, the validity of the estimates of the transition probabilities was increased considerably. Pauses and transition probabilities appear in consequence mutually related: predictability i.e. high transition probability (or redundancy) and fluency being as closely linked as pauses and uncertainty of prediction (or entropy).

Pauses have thus been shown not only to anticipate a sudden increase in information, but their interpolation seems to be a necessary condition for such an increase. The difficulty of investing the concept of information as coined by Shannon (1951) i.e. a statistical entity, with a meaning or semantic content, has frequently been discussed. The present investigation is relevant to this problem for the following reasons:

It started with a hypothesis conceived in psychological terms which, on analysis of the problem, led to a reformulation in information theory language. The resulting hypothesis, that the function of pauses is to increase information, was confirmed (to start with) at the statistical level.

It was shown that the hesitation pauses, an aspect of behaviour of speakers, presumably related to a subjective state of the speaking organism, were related to an aspect of objective language, namely transition probabilities dependent on word frequency in the language at large, linguistic structure and context.

We have seen that fluent speech consisted of sequences of words which were easily predicted from the context by guessers who knew nothing about the original speaker's intentions in respect of these sequences. In other words, the combinations between the words in such sequences were shared by the language community. They proved to be of the nature of verbal habits within the linguistic group, with the result that their pairing had been learned and become more or less automatic. In most of these cases, however, where guessers found themselves at a loss for predicting the next word as spoken originally, i.e. where the sequence ceased to be a matter of common conditioning or learning, the original speaker also seemed to have been at a loss for the next word, for it was at these points that he tended to hesitate. The language he produced after the pause was difficult or even impossible to predict, for the guesser knew nothing of his intentions. The original speaker's choice was highly individual and was unexpected (being made anew at the time of speaking). It was created for the occasion and fitted to a specific meaning content of his own.

Fluency and hesitation thus help us to discriminate between two kinds of speech. Experimentally it was possible to differentiate them in terms of low and high transition probability. Functionally they appear to coincide with Jackson's division of speech into automatic and voluntary, or "old, well organized" and "new, now organizing" speech.

The behaviour of fluency and hesitation in speech seems therefore to signalize the originality of choice, the novelty of the language as produced on the one hand, and the habit strength by which links in verbal sequences are associated on the other hand. This is the case, however, only if speech is truly spontaneous, i.e. if it is generated afresh, if the speaker is thinking on his feet. We shall see in a later experiment how, once spontaneity is gone out of speech, the objective measure of expectancy, i.e. the information content of the language, ceases to reflect the subjective act of choice, of decision making in the speaker. It still is information to the listener (has its "surprise" effect, its news value) but it has become separated from the creative act of generating speech.

The relation between response latency and response uncertainty, and reaction time, has exercised a number of workers and W. R. Garner

(1962) in discussing these studies concludes that the critical point in the relation between reaction time and amount of uncertainty is the factor of response conflict: with a great deal of learning, where there is little response conflict, the relation between stimulus uncertainty and reaction time is flattened out.

The behaviour of pausing (or uttering speech fluently) on the other hand indicates—under all conditions—whether the process in the brain is a generative one or one of associative linkage. In other words there is no mechanical relation between information and hesitation in speech nor indeed can there be between information and delay generally. The relation must be channelled via the internal process, the cognitive act and its substructures in the nervous system which are involved in generating speech. Objective properties of the language can be expected to reflect mental effort during the course of its creation only, but not after practice. Indeed it is the hallmark of all practice and all skill that it retains the fruits of effort (which in language is a high content of information), while dispensing with the effort itself.

Having tested our hypothesis that pausing indicates cognitive activity by relating it to information under spontaneous conditions and having recognized hesitation pauses as the "now" periods of speech organization, we proceed to use pause behaviour as an indicator in its own rights to sort out which parts of verbal sequences are verbal habits and which are being created at the time of speaking; we now propose to state with some precision at which point in the encoding process that part of it which organizes speech takes place.

The concept of information in the situation of spontaneous encoding has thus been shown to be capable of extension beyond its statistical frame of reference; it has been shown to include the semantic aspect of choice, or organization of specific linguistic solutions to fit certain meaning contents intended for verbalization.

Its semantic significance has become evident when the probability structure derived from common usage was confronted with the process of the creation of individual speech or of instantaneous organization of speech in specific structures. A more direct relation between the transition probability of words and the semantic complexity of the texts containing them will be reported in detail later (p. 62).

The results of the experiments described also indicate that the forward course of speech production is affected by the probability structure of subsequent as well as preceding speech. Fluency in the production of external speech in sentences consequently appears to be a function of their linguistic structure, whether already implemented or yet to be verbalized.

This effect cannot be explained by the assumption of mere associative linkage of elements in sequences. It is on the other hand much better understood if we make the assumption of duality of the speech process as expounded by Jackson (1878), which was described in Chapter 1. It may be recalled that according to this view, every action is based on an anticipatory plan possessing a specific structure. Jackson conceives of the process of verbalization (as of action generally) as occurring in duplicate, each operation being completed subjectively before it is carried out objectively. The "subject-proposition" precedes the "object-proposition".

In the light of this hypothesis hesitation pauses in speech may be conceived of as indicating the lag between subjective and objective, planning and execution or between the central and the peripheral processes. In old and acquired forms of speech where the process is automatic and the first half of it subconscious, speech is highly integrated and utterance, i.e. peripheral speech, instantaneous.

Where the words are being fitted to the proposition anew, the lag between the central act of planning and the peripheral act of vocal action was expected to be a function of the degree of indecision in selecting the words to be fitted.

So far the experiments reported here have only been concerned with the incidence of pauses irrespective of their duration. The contingency that the various degrees of indecision and disintegration between the central and peripheral parts of the verbalizing process are reflected in the duration of pauses was examined in the following experiments.

(b) Duration of Pauses, Information and Meaning

EXPERIMENT

The following experiment (Goldman-Eisler, 1958c) was designed to ascertain whether the amount of information content is related to the duration of pauses made by readers who extemporized missing words in sentences originally uttered by someone else. If such a relationship were to exist, the earlier conclusion would be corroborated.

MATERIAL

The material of this experiment consisted of four sentences recorded from spontaneous speech. The duration of the hesitation pauses was measured and the amount of information content in the words was determined in terms of their transition probabilities.

The sentences were subjected to two different treatments:

(1) Each sentence was prepared for the experimental subjects by substituting blanks for the words with high information content.

(2) Each sentence was also prepared by substituting blanks for words with low information content.

These alterations were carried out so that the number of actual words in each corresponding pair of sentences was equal and so that the gaps between the words were fairly distributed. Since words of high and low information tended to alternate, the processing of the sentences was surprisingly easy.

EXPERIMENTAL PROCEDURE

The instructions to the subjects were that they were to read the sentences aloud and substitute for the blanks the words they thought most suitable in the context. Proceeding at a conversational pace, they were to visualize an imaginary listener waiting for the sentence to come to an end within a reasonable time.

The design of the experiment so ordered the presentation of the two types of sentences that both the effects of learning and the influence of the order of presentation were eliminated. Eight subjects participated.

The reading and completion of blanks was recorded on tape, and a pen recorder on teledeltos paper indicated the durations of periods of speech and silence. These recordings made it possible to measure the durations of the interrupting pauses with some precision (0·1 sec). The rate of reading and completion was calculated, in syllables per sec, from the total duration of each reading.

RESULTS

(1) Where the gaps stood for words of low information content, the mean length of hesitation before substituting words for the blanks was 20 sec; where the gaps stood for words of high information content, the comparable mean length was 37 sec. This difference is significant at the level of $p=0·01$ $(F=8·8)$ but some of the variance (significant at the 0·05 level) was between sentences. The individual differences among readers were of little consequence in determining the length of the hesitations. Thus the amount of information which a word contains is related to the length of hesitation when a reader fills blanks; the shortest hesitations occur when words contain the least amount of information (as defined earlier, a word is low in information content if subjects find it easy to predict it on the basis of the preceding portion of the sentence).

(2) The time which the subjects took to fill the blanks varied widely (between 1 and 92 sec) and their duration obviously differed from that of the pauses of the speakers who had originally produced the sentences spontaneously. A comparison of the length of pauses of the speakers with those of the readers showed that a positive and significant relationship $(\chi^2 =6·0$ and $6·1; p =0·02)$ existed for two of the sentences. Thus for

two sentences the completion of gaps concealing words originally preceded by pauses required a significantly longer period of hesitation than the filling of blanks for words uttered fluently. For the other two sentences no such relationship existed. A further analysis suggests an explanation for these seemingly contradictory results. It showed that there were considerable differences in the proportion of words correctly substituted for blanks even within the same treatment groups: substitution was easy or difficult within each treatment group. This is illustrated in Table 7 which shows the two treatment groups divided into:

(a) those where the readers' delays were proportional to the original speakers' pauses and
(b) those where no such relationship was evident.

TABLE 7

Percentages of correct words inserted in sentences showing a relationship between original speakers' and readers' pauses when blanks stood for words of high and low information content (H).

Treatment groups	Percentages of correct words in sentences	
	(a) With pause relationship	(b) Without pause relationship
1 (Blanks for words of high H)	40%	13%
2 (Blanks for words of low H)	80%	55%

DISCUSSION

In interpreting these results the act of duplicating the original wording may be understood as follows: a high proportion of correct words indicates that the sentence schema of the reader was similar to that which had determined the word choice of the original speaker; that, in other words, the lines of meaning which guided the reader's verbal thinking and those guiding the thinking of the original speaker were the same. On the other hand, a low proportion of correct choices in completing the experimental sentences indicates that the reader found it difficult to anticipate the direction of the original speaker's thinking.

Thus, readers filling blanks in incomplete sentences have a significantly greater chance of approximating the original version whenever the sentence schema presented allows for a reconstruction of the meaning according to the intention of the original speaker. Further, the lengths of the hesitations of subjects who thought along the same lines as the original speaker were positively related to the lengths of the pauses of the original speech. In those sentences, on the other hand, in which the omission of words reduced information content to the extent that meaningful reconstruction was obstructed, no relation existed between the length of the pauses by readers and those by the original speakers. Those who think alike thus appear to behave alike in the matter of pauses.

A relation appears to exist between periods of hesitation before verbalization in different persons performing different operations within the same linguistic setting. The condition under which this relation was seen to hold is one characterized by successful anticipation of the original speaker's intentions.

The previous experiment (Goldman-Eisler, 1958b) established a relation between pausing (an aspect of the behaviour of speakers) and information content (an aspect of linguistic structure), but the present result goes further. This new study shows that different individuals, provided that they are operating on the same language material and are thinking within identical areas of meaning, will respond in terms of their fluency of speech in a similar way to the tasks of creating speech and of reconstructing this same speech from fragments. An understanding of the significance of this finding depends upon a consideration of the implications of these two linguistic acts.

CONCLUSION

The earlier experiment concluded that the process of verbalization consists of two parts and that every act of speech is based on an anticipatory plan possessing a specific structure. Hesitation pauses then indicate a lag between the two halves of the verbalizing process, the central and the peripheral or the formation of the concept and the act of phonation. In (Jackson's) "old and acquired forms of speech", where the central process becomes both automatic and subconscious, the physical production of speech is highly integrated and utterances are instantaneous. When the words are being fitted to the proposition anew, on the other hand, hesitations in verbalization are a function of the degree of uncertainty involved in selecting the appropriate words.

An application of the preceding hypothesis to the results of the present experiment equates the task of completing the experimental sentences to the peripheral stage of the verbalizing process in spontaneous speech. The fact that the durations of pauses in reading and spontaneous speaking were related when the reader successfully anticipated the intentions of the original speaker seems to indicate that both types of pause—those made by the original speaker in spontaneous speech and those made by the subject in the experiment completing the blanks in the same sentences—are, in fact, identical in function, i.e. they are related to the selection of words to be fitted into an existing structure.

The fact that the durations of pauses in the completion task and in spontaneous speaking were not related when the reader failed to anticipate the intentions of the original speaker indicates that in the absence of such knowledge word selection through sequential dependencies breaks down. Thus, the statistical determination of speech appears as only one factor in its production, and there must presumably be other factors which account for the generation of the content and for the creation of the framework of grammatical structure within which the substance is verbalized; further, content and organization are shown to be primary and their generation to precede lexical selection.

Summary to Chapter 2

This chapter contains the description of experiments which were designed to examine the function of hesitation pauses in speech. Specifically pauses were conceived of as anticipating increase of information in subsequent speech and as involving acts of choice.

This hypothesis was tested by relating the incidence of pauses within sentences to the transition probabilities of the words constituting them. Estimates of these probabilities were obtained experimentally by an adaptation of Shannon's guessing technique and were based on reverse as well as forward guessing. The hypothesis was borne out by the facts: hesitancy in speech was shown to be closely related to uncertainty of prediction and fluency of utterance to redundancy. These results were also shown to be in line with the facts of language statistics.

The fact that the forward left-to-right progression of external speech, and its degree of fluency or hesitancy, is affected by the ties that link words not only to what preceded but also to what is yet to come was interpreted to mean that fluency in the production of external speech in sentences is not entirely a function of the unit-by-unit strength of the word sequence, i.e. a matter of learning connections. It was taken to suggest that pausing was also related to the language structure whether already implemented or yet to be verbalized. The assumption of a mere linkage of associated elements in sequence was rejected as incompatible with the facts obtained. It was proposed that the production of external speech should be viewed as the result of at least two simultaneous processes, one concerned with planning the content and grammatical structure and the other with word choice to fit this structure. The spoken sentence would then be the final utterance of the temporal sequence in which the verbal material had been organized.

An otherwise unintelligible result of a further experiment became plausible with the assumption of a syntactic-plus-semantic frame-work. This experiment was designed to re-create the conditions for word selection in sentences originally uttered spontaneously through a sentence completion task.

This turned out to be successful where the subject was able to anticipate the trend and meaning of sentences and unsuccessful where no such anticipation was evident. In the former case, the time of pausing when re-creating the complete sentences from their skeletons was proportional to the original speaker's pausing time, in the latter no such relation was found.

Chapter 3

The Semantic Determination of Pauses and Spontaneity

Having seen how decisive a knowledge of the speaker's intentions, i.e. semantic information, is in facilitating lexical choices, we cannot but suspect that the cognitive effort that goes into the formulation of speech utterances and results in the totality of a verbal statement must, to a large extent, be spent at the semantic level.

Therefore, if pausing accompanies cognitive operations, we expect that this semantic effort be reflected in the pausing of speakers.

To test this proposition an experiment was required in which the construction of meaning and the generation of semantic content were indispensable as were controlled operations in the generation of speech while spontaneity was still fully preserved.

In designing such an experiment one has to take care also to create conditions for verbal activity made to stimulate content decisions so that they are subject to different degrees of constraint or freedom. If we require speakers to talk on some definite subject or, more widely, within some field of discourse, they are constrained in what they can say. The extent of such a constraint may vary; for instance the instruction to describe a course of events is constraining in a much higher degree than the instruction to interpret their meaning, the former enforcing greater conformity, the latter allowing greater divergence. In the first case, in description, verbalization involves verbal representation of serially connected phenomena in the same sequence as they are experienced. Interpretation, i.e. abstracting a meaning from events and formulating it verbally, requires an attitude of detachment from the concrete situation—from the events as perceived and their mental reorganization. Thus the process of encoding is raised to a higher level of symbolic representation or, in the terms of information theory, serially connected information is recoded with less redundancy.

A second aim of this experiment was to study hesitation pauses under different conditions of spontaneity. The relation shown to exist (Goldman-Eisler, 1958b) between hesitation and information, or fluency and redundancy, of speech (i.e. between properties of behaviour and properties of language) was demonstrated in a sample of spontaneous speech; the inference was that well-learned, well-organized and familiar sequences of speech, though linguistically identical, would not exhibit such a relationship, if hesitation is to be taken as behaviour which is synchronous with, and indicative of, encoding processes responsible for generation of information.

The Experiment

Several series of cartoon stories without captions, of the kind regularly published in *The New Yorker*, were shown to the subjects (see Fig. 11). These cartoons are distinguished by the fact that they confine themselves to a completely pictorial code and usually have a somewhat subtle point or carry some kind of moral, the deducing of which requires generalization.

In the experiment to be described in detail nine such cartoons were selected from *The New Yorker* and presented to nine subjects each in varying order. Subsequently more such experiments (Goldman-Eisler *et al.*, 1965) were performed, with the same results. The subjects were instructed as follows:

"You will be shown a series of cartoon stories with no verbal captions.

Fig. 11A Drawing by Claude; © 1957 The New Yorker Magazine, Inc.

You are asked to have a good look at them. As soon as you have got
the point say 'Got it' and proceed to describe the content of the story
as depicted in the pictures before you; conclude by formulating the
general point, meaning or moral of the story in as concise a form as you
can. There is no time limit, and you may keep the pictures to look at

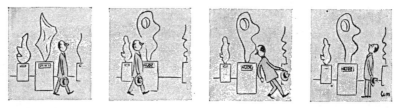

FIG. 11B Drawing by CEM; © 1957 The New Yorker Magazine Inc.

all through the experiment. Repeat this several times until I stop you.
If you are not satisfied with your first version you have the opportunity
to improve or modify it in the repetitions, but stick to the first reasonable version, and then keep repeating the same wording."

FIG. 11C Drawing by F. B. Modell; © 1957 The New Yorker Magazine, Inc.

The subjects were asked to repeat six times. Altogether there were seven editions of each description and interpretation, which seemed sufficient to render the process automatic.

The subjects' remarks were recorded on a tape-recorder from the moment the experimenter handed them the cartoon page with the words, "Look at these please" to the end of their formulation of the point.

The experiment was thus designed to give a gradation along the scale leading from newly planned and formulated speech action to routine, automatic action (given through the repetition of the original version). This gradation was to occur at two distinctly different levels of verbal behaviour; that of description of concrete events and of the interpretation of their meaning abstracted from them. Spontaneity of speech in descriptions must therefore be understood to be of a different class from spontaneity when interpreting meaning.

At the first, spontaneous stage of the experiment (the original description and interpretation), the activity stimulated may be imagined to involve a series of transformations.

(1) The first involves the intake and decoding of the pictorial information. This is not a language problem. The reception of the message is via the visual channel and is not verbally explicit. It is presumably in two steps, the first being the intake of the pictures in sequence and the second the grasp of their significance.

(2) The second transformation involves the representation of sequences of events suggested by the visual symbols perceived in the form of language symbols. The information is encoded in the same sequence as it was decoded.

(3) The third set of transformations involves the explicit abstraction and verbal formulation of the meaning of the cartoons. Sequential information is reorganized and recoded into the form of a general maxim. Association by contiguity is transformed into association by similarity. This formulation will be referred to as the interpretation.

The number of pictures in each cartoon story varied from one to eight. The various considerations determining the choice of cartoons for the experiment made it difficult to keep the number of pictures constant. Intelligibility and an implied but deducible meaning were considered to be more important criteria of selection. In the first attempt 4579 words were produced by nine subjects in describing all nine cartoons and 1063 in interpreting their meaning. Including the six repetitions, 29,157 words were uttered in describing and 9212 in interpreting the cartoons. Individual differences were highly significant. The mean output for subjects ranged between 31 and 92 words for descriptions and 7 to 27 words for interpretations.

TREATMENT OF DATA

The sound recordings were transformed into a visual record as described before, the speech on the magnetic tape was then synchronized with these visual records and measurements were made from them of the following quantities:

(1) Period of intake (taken from "Look at these" to "got it").
(2) Initial delay of description (period from "Got it" to words of description).
(3) Duration of description (taken from "Got it" to its last word).
(4) Duration of interpretation (starting from the last word of description and taken to its last word).
(5) Length of pauses in descriptions.
(6) Length of pauses in interpretation.
(7) Number of words in description.
(8) Number of words in interpretation.

From these quantities were derived the measures of (a) total duration of pauses in descriptions and interpretations and (b) total duration of talking in descriptions and in interpretations.

MEASURES OF HESITATION

There are various ways of expressing the degree of hesitation in speech. If duration of pauses is the basic quantity it must be related to the length of the utterance whose degree of hesitation (or whose hesitancy) is to be measured. In any speech sequence pause and speech periods usually alternate in an irregular and seemingly unsystematic fashion. Naturally, pauses accumulate and with increasing length of utterance, the total pause time also increases. Hesitancy is therefore a ratio of pause time to speech time, if by speech we refer to vocal action only. The total amount of speech can be measured either as the total duration of the vocal activity in the utterance, or be expressed by the number of words, syllables or letters produced in it. The latter quantity has the advantage of allowing the elimination of irrelevant vocal productions, i.e. noise, such as repetitions of the same words or other obvious forms of marking time vocally. In this way the pause time is brought more closely into relation with the information content of speech. A measure of this kind was obtained by calculating the ratio of the pause time of an utterance to the words produced in it (P/W).

RESULTS 1

The total amount of hesitation in describing the cartoons was expressed in terms of the total duration of pausing; that is, by the sum of individual pause periods of the sequence between the signal "Got it" and the last word of the description. For the interpretations, the hesitation was expressed in terms of the sum of pause periods from the last word of the description to the last word of the interpretation.

The ratios of pause time to speech time, or relative hesitancy in descriptions and interpretations, differ considerably. This can be seen from Table 8 which lists the mean lengths (over nine cartoons) of total periods of descriptions (D) and interpretations (*I*) for nine subjects and of periods of talking and silence separately.

TABLE 8
Means for nine subjects

Subjects	Total length of descriptions and interpretations sec		Total length of speech periods sec		Total length of pause periods		Relative hesitancy = pause/speech ratio	
	D	I	D	I	D	I	D	I
Th	21·1	13·7	12·7	4·2	6·3	9·2	0·50	2·17
Ha	39·0	13·6	16·1	2·9	22·9	10·3	1·43	3·57
Tr	42·6	28·5	12·9	5·3	29·7	22·0	2·33	4·17
Wi	25·5	13·7	12·9	5·9	12·5	7·9	0·97	1·33
Sa	65·1	21·4	29·2	4·8	35·9	16·6	1·23	3·45
Gi	37·3	22·1	19·7	10·6	16·9	12·2	0·86	1·15
Ne	25·3	19·4	11·4	8·1	12·8	10·2	1·12	1·27
Au	79·9	24·1	20·8	9·1	29·1	14·8	1·39	1·64
Do	21·8	9·3	9·2	3·1	12·6	6·2	1·37	2·00
Great mean	39·2	18·4	16·1	6·0	20·0	12·2	1·24	3·31

The relative hesitancy, as expressed by the ratio of total pause time to total speech time, was significantly larger for interpretations (2·31 on average) than for descriptions (average of 1·24). While the actual vocal activity of speaking in descriptions took (on average) 2·75 times as long as the speech output in the interpretations, hesitation (the total amount of pausing that went with it) was only 1·62 times as long. In other words, there was more pausing for the same amount of speech when subjects had to formulate the meaning of the cartoons than when they had to describe them. The difference was highly significant ($t = 3·60$, p for one-tailed test less than 0·005). Individual differences also played an important role, but an analysis of variance (based on the measure of pause length per word produced P/W) showed that while individual differences were the main factor in determining variation in hesitancy within the same verbal assignment, the variance due to the difference in verbal task (description and interpretation) was significantly greater ($p = 0·025$) than that due to individual differences.

RESULTS 2

There was a distinct tendency for subjects to delay the first utterance of a description as well as of an interpretation. It seems not unlikely that this initial delay might more specifically be concerned with the content and structural decisions than with lexical decisions; with the latter, presumably only as far as the first continuous word sequence was concerned. The comparison of the total hesitancy, as shown above, gives a non-specific picture of relative total effort in the verbal formulation of descriptions and interpretations. To gain a more specific picture these total durations were divided into (a) pause time accumulating between first and last word, which will be referred to as *within sentence* pauses (of descriptions as well as of interpretations) and (b) *initial delays*.

TABLE 9
Means for nine subjects

Subjects	Initial pauses sec		Within-sentence pauses sec		Within-sentence hesitancy (pause to speech ratio)	
	D	I	D	I	D	I
Th	4·0	2·6	2·3	6·6	0·18	1·62
Ha	8·3	6·2	14·6	4·1	0·91	1·44
Tr	8·5	10·2	21·2	11·8	1·64	2·22
Wi	3·8	2·3	8·7	5·6	0·69	1·05
Sa	10·0	10·1	25·9	6·5	0·89	1·35
Gi	4·6	3·6	12·3	8·6	0·62	0·81
Ne	3·9	2·2	8·9	8·0	0·78	0·99
Au	4·4	1·9	24·7	12·9	0·85	1·41
Do	4·9	3·1	7·7	3·1	0·84	1·00

(a) *Within-sentence Hesitancy.* The ratios of the lengths of within-sentence pauses to actual speech durations, for descriptions and interpretations separately, was calculated and will be referred to as *within-sentence hesitancy*. From the figures given in Table 9 we can see that the within-sentence hesitancy is constantly less in verbal tasks involving description of perceived events, than those requiring, through the interpretation of their meaning, their recoding. The difference is significant ($t = 3·82$, p less than 0·005 one tail).

(b) *Initial Delays.* The initial delays will be dealt with in Chapter 4.

Hesitation, Spontaneity and Practice

RESULTS 3

These results show the hesitancy under different conditions of spontaneity. Pause length per word was calculated from the quantities measured for each repetition of descriptions and interpretations (see Fig. 12).

Two facts may be worth noting:

(1) The sudden decrease in hesitancy after the first, original versions and the subsequent gradual decrease from the first to the sixth repetition point to a qualitative difference between the original verbalization and its repetition.

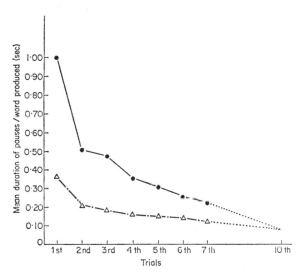

FIG. 12 Hesitancy at two levels of verbal planning and its decrease with repetition
Δ = Description, $\bullet$ = interpretation.

(2) With practice, the discrepancy in fluency between descriptions and interpretations is reduced.

It is clear from this that differences of information contained in speech, such as we meet in descriptions and interpretations, are reflected in hesitation behaviour only when the speaker is in the process of and is presently generating the information. *Hesitation is thus shown to be an indicator of the internal act of generating information rather than of the statistical predictability of the linguistic expression. In line with the expectation, as soon as this becomes habituated, the link between hesitation and information disappears.*

CONCLUSION

If the production of all speech were of equal difficulty, the time taken for the utterance of statements would, for any individual, be completely

C

determined by the quantity of speech units uttered; whatever the verbal task, fluency would be constant. This, as we have seen, is not the case; pause length per word increases considerably as we pass from describing concrete events to interpreting their general meaning.

Previously, length of hesitation pauses within sentences had been shown (Goldman-Eisler, 1958b) to be a function of the predictability of the words following them. In the present investigation two types of hesitation were studied, initial delays as well as within-sentence hesitations. At every step in the psycholinguistic continuum, preliminary to, as well as concomitant with, the vocal utterance, the interpretation of meaning i.e. abstracting and generalizing from perceived events requires more time in pausing than does their description.

It is thus evident that the statistical aspect of language, by which we mean the predictability of words in context, is only one factor in the determination of the hesitancy or fluency of speech. Level of abstraction and scope of generalization in generating content have emerged as the second factor. In subjective terms the two factors translate into lexical choices and complex semantic creation.

Summary to Chapter 3

The assumption that hesitation pauses in speech are the delays due to processes taking place in the brain whenever speech ceases to be the automatic vocalization of learned sequences, whether occasioned by choice of an individual word, by construction of syntax, or by conception of content, led to the experiment described in this chapter. It was designed to make thought construction an indispensable and controlled part of the speaking process. This was achieved by presenting subjects with the task of describing as well as interpreting the meaning of cartoons.

The experiment also provided for a scaling from spontaneity to automatic action, and from production to reproduction. It was designed to give a gradation along the scale leading from newly formulated speech to routine, automatic speech action given through the repetition of the original version. This was obtained for the description of the content as well as the interpretations of the meaning of the cartoons.

The results showed that pausing time when speakers interpreted meaning was about twice as much as when they described content. Pausing also varied with the different degrees of spontaneity. There was

a sudden decline after the first trial and a gradual decrease of pausing in the subsequent repetitions. This was taken to indicate that the
difference between spontaneity and reiteration, between production
and reproduction, is a qualitative one, reflecting the dual nature of
psycholinguistic operations.

Chapter 4

Complexity of Cognitive Operations and Information and Hesitation

The difference in pause behaviour, between production and reproduction of language illustrated in Fig. 12 (p. 57), shows very clearly that the differences in cognitive complexity are reflected in pausing only when the language is generated while the utterance is being organized. How is this global semantic complexity related to the information content of the component words?

(1) Is the complexity of cognitive operations reflected in the predictability of the words generated? To answer this question, transition probabilities were estimated as before, playing the Shannon game left to right and right to left (743 words and 43 sentences were involved—479 words and 24 sentences in the descriptions and 255 words and 19 sentences in the interpretations). When the words contained were divided into fluent and hesitant (i.e. preceded by a pause) the mean transition probability, whether produced for the first time or after practice, was as follows:

0·45 for fluent descriptions (D_F)
0·37 for hesitant descriptions (D_H)
0·34 for fluent interpretations (I_F)
0·28 for hesitant interpretations (I_H)

Table 10 shows the ratios of words of low to words of high transition probability for the four groups: in low are included words of not more than $P = 0·2$, and in high, words of 0·8 to 1·0.

TABLE 10
Ratios of low (0 to 0·2) to high (0·8 to 1·0)
transition probabilities

	Fluent speech	Hesitant speech	Total
Descriptions	1·57	3·00	1·85
Interpretations	4·89	9·50	5·73

Predicting individual words in sentences describing cartoons was, according to these figures, easier all round than predicting words in sentences used to interpret their meaning. When interpreting the guessers found more words difficult and less words easy to predict, even where the original speaker attained the same degree of fluency as in the descriptions. There is little difference between the transition probability for D_H (0·37) and I_F (0·34). That level differences (D and I) were more basic is borne out by the fact that although transition probabilities discriminated significantly between fluent and hesitant words in the descriptions (D_F and D_H) ($C\chi^2 = 6\cdot5$, $P < 0\cdot01$), this was not the case with the words used in the case of interpretations ($\chi^2 = 1\cdot07$).

(2) The question might be raised here why I_F words carried more information than D_F words as judging from absence of pauses both categories seemed to require little generative effort. The setting of the material in this investigation of sentences subjected to transitional analysis was such that the F and H categories were based on within sentence hesitations. The full records, on the other hand, showed periods of initial delays before utterance of descriptions or interpretations was started. Although subjects were asked to proceed with the descriptions and interpretations immediately after apprehending the point and after the description to carry on formulating the interpretation, most speech action was started after some delay.

Initial Delays

These initial delays (measured separately) constituted a considerable proportion of total pause time, being an average of 31 % for the descriptions and of 43 % for the summaries.

TABLE 11

Periods of intake of meaning of cartoons

Cartoon	Means for cartoons sec	Means for subjects	sec
Man and girl become engaged	42·9	Th	20·2
Wishing well	20·0	Ha	18·7
Court jester and king	15·5	Tr	22·4
Modern sculpture	12·2	Wi	14·9
Traffic signs	14·1	Sa	39·5
Psychiatrist and patient	14·7	Gi	15·4
Psychiatrist and woman patient	22·0	Ne	14·9
Artist and painting saved	11·2	Au	14·2
Woman buys antique	20·6	Do	13·0

Table 11 shows the mean durations of the intake of the cartoons (apprehension period from "Look" to "Got it") and Table 9 (Column 1), the durations of the initial delays of descriptions and interpretations; (these are indicated by the letters D and I). We shall refer to these three silences as apprehension or intake period, initial delay D and initial delay I, the latter two being anticipatory hesitations to distinguish them from the pauses within the utterances or within-sentences hesitations. As the point of the cartoons had been grasped at the close of the intake period, when the subjects gave the signal "Got it" to mark this fact, the initial delays must be considered to be oriented towards the subsequent utterances.

Judging from their position in relation to the whole sentence they should be much more heavily weighted with the activity of generating content and organizing grammatical structure than the within-sentence pauses which one would expect to be concerned more with lexical decisions. Their average duration for descriptions (5·9 sec) exceeded that for the interpretations (5·0 sec) by only a little, considering the large difference in speech output (55·8 words on the average for descriptions and 16·3 words for interpretations). In other words, it took about the same time for speakers to organize themselves to the point of starting utterances of an average length of 55·8 words when describing events, as it took to begin the formulation of interpretations of a length of 16·3.

This would indicate that the 16 words in the interpretations contained about the same amount of information (H) as the 56 words of the descriptions. It would mean that lexical choice becomes more difficult in proportion to the increase in the complexity of general planning. Semantic complexity, one might speculate on this basis, may be something indivisible, a quality of language realized in the words chosen; in this sense the principle of the unity of form and content seems to manifest itself.

(3) The subjects were asked to recode the descriptions concisely and without redundancy. The fluency of words in their interpretations must be seen against this background, i.e. that of the long initial delay. One might recall here Lashley's description of aggregates of words partially activated and held in check before the sentence order is imposed on them in expression.

Hesitation and Economy in Expression

Conciseness or brevity of expression is popularly valued as a better or more elegant form of verbal expression than prolixity. It is a matter of popular belief that concise statements are the fruit of greater mental labour than discursive ones. Within the terms of the present investigation, conciseness or brevity of expression would be expected to be a function of its hesitancy. The assumption underlying this expectation is that a reduction in amount of speech did not involve a reduction of information.

In relating the mean quantities for hesitancy and speech output, no correlation was found for the descriptions, but there was a significant negative correlation $(r = -0·683)$ for the interpretations. The more hesitant the speaker, the shorter was his formulation of the meaning of the cartoons.

The relation showed itself to hold not only for the means between the subjects, but also for the interpretations produced for the nine cartoons

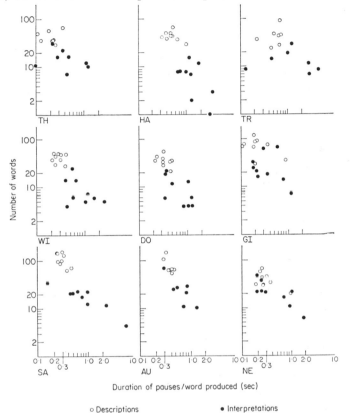

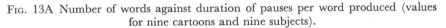

Duration of pauses/word produced (sec)

o Descriptions   • Interpretations

FIG. 13A Number of words against duration of pauses per word produced (values for nine cartoons and nine subjects).

by each individual (see Figs. 13A and 13B). Within their own individual range, subjects tended to utter their more concise formulations with greater hesitancy, while where they were fluent in utterance they tended to be more long-winded in formulation.

However, while hesitancy is consistently inversely related to the quantity of speech produced in the interpretations, it is independent of it in the descriptions. A Chi-square based on associated probabilities (Fisher, 1938) was not significant (Chi-square $= 19 \cdot 68$, $df = 18$, $p = 0 \cdot 50$) for the latter, and highly significant (Chi-square $= 32 \cdot 30$, $df = 18$ $p = 0 \cdot 02$) for the former.

Our data confirm the assumption that brevity of formulation, where

brevity is desired, is an achievement at least in the sense that it takes
more time to attain it and it is in this sense more difficult.

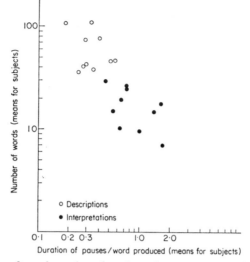

FIG. 13B Number of words against duration of pauses per word produced (means
for subjects).

Hesitation and Intellectual Quality

Brevity as an aspect of quality, a manifestation of conciseness of expression, is a property of style and the question of the intellectual
quality of the various cartoon interpretations was still left open. In
view of the nature of the task, the main criterion of the intellectual
quality had to be degree or universality of the generalization. Another
criterion was relevance of interpretations to the story of the cartoons, a
minimum requirement without which degree of generalization was
meaningless. By generalization we understand an act of thought by
which meaning is derived from the data of experience, e.g. by extending

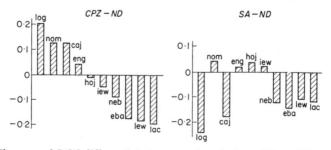

FIG. 14 Changes of P/W differentials between descriptions (D) and interpretations
(I) from No Drug to Chlorpromazine (CPZ-ND) and Sodium Amytal (SA-ND) for
10 subjects.

the significance of the cartoons from the particular to a multitude of instances. In the same sense Vygotsky (1962) takes generalization to mean the formation of a superordinate that includes the given concept as a particular case.

The elucidation of this question became necessary in order to understand the results of an experiment (Goldman-Eisler *et al.*, 1965) in which adult and highly intelligent subjects after being injected with Chlorpromazine showed changes in their pause behaviour which were difficult to interpret. As before speech was evoked at two levels of complexity represented in the descriptions and interpretations of *The New Yorker* cartoons.

The purpose of these experiments was to find how far the known effect of Chlorpromazine in depressing arousal and reducing vigilance was reflected in complex cognitive processes as indicated by hesitation pauses. The measure used was the differential of P/W between the two tasks (this difference of P/W will be referred to as P). This additional time of pausing seemed apposite as a criterion of increased vigilance by virtue of its reflecting increase in effort and application to the task when passing from the easier one of describing to the more difficult intellectual task of interpreting the cartoons.

The effect of Chlorpromazine on pausing time in the interpretations of cartoons proved to be selective and varying in direction with individuals. Some subjects showed dramatic reductions, whilst others increased the amount of their pausing (see Fig. 14).

Sodium amytal was also administered to these subjects but its action where it was effective was uni-directional (see Table 12).

TABLE 12

Changes of P/W differentials between descriptions (D) and Interpretations (I) from no drug to chlorpromazine $(CPZ—ND)$ and sodium amytal $(SA—ND)$ conditions (for ten subjects)

Subjects	$CPZ—ND$	$SA—ND$
lac	0·194	0·117
log	0·199	0·242
nom	0·126	0·045
lew	0·183	0·109
neb	0·088	0·122
eba	0·174	0·144
caj	0·126	0·180
erg	0·041	0·020
iew	0·047	0·021
hoj	0·011	0·038

The selective action of Chlorpromazine raised the questions:

(1) How to interpret gain or loss in the pause differential between two verbal tasks (P) of different cognitive complexity? Is the gain in time efficient in terms of gain in conceptual quality or is it inefficient and unproductive?

Under normal conditions a delay of speech action would be interpreted, with reference to the evidence at hand, as a signal that cognitive processes were taking place, and such delay would be assumed to be likely to result in cognitive achievement. To extrapolate this conclusion to the functioning of a brain under the influence of a drug seemed unwarranted.

(2) Can we take it that we are dealing with a selective action of Chlorpromazine in accordance with some aspects of personality, in which case Chlorpromazine would be maximizing individual differences in a systematic way? (Here we shall concentrate on question 1; question 2 will reappear in the second part of this volume.)

Assessment of Intellectual Quality

To assess the intellectual quality of the interpretations, an experiment (Goldman-Eisler, 1964a) was carried out in which independent judges were used who were kept unaware about the conditions or subjects in the experiment.

One hundred and eighty statements formulating the meaning of the cartoons had been made by 10 subjects under the 3 conditions: No Drug, Chlorpromazine and Sodium amytal. These were typed out on cards and arranged so that all those statements referring to the same cartoon were grouped together. Three judges—senior academic staff, University College London—were presented separately with the relevant cartoons and all the associated statements and were asked to rate the statements (using a four-point scale) according to these two criteria:

(a) Generalization
   Is the statement a recoding or reformulation of the cartoon stories in general terms so as to be inclusive of a larger variety of specific instances?
(b) Relevance
   Is the statement apposite to the cartoon?

This latter question (b) was used to provide a check as to whether the reformulation in general terms was meaningful, rather than used as a criterion of cognitive level. Statements of poor generality, such as recapitulations of the concrete story, would be relevant and yet be complete failures as far as the required task (formulating meaning or point) was concerned. Thus relevance by itself constituted no point in favour of the subject. The reason why it was introduced was to sort out generalizations which had no bearing on the story itself, for it was conceivable for subjects to use some kind of ill-fitted cliché without satisfying the experimental requirement for generalization. This, however, occurred so rarely that we can concentrate on degree of generalization (against a common background of relevance) as the crucial criterion of cognitive level.

The relation between increase in pausing and improvement in interpretations as voted by the judges was highly significant between Chlorpromazine and No Drug ($p = 0.0027$) but not significant between Sodium amytal and No Drug ($p = 0.1515$). In other words, changes in the P/W differential (P) as compared with No Drug were correlated with changes in the quality of the interpretations from No Drug to Chlorpromazine—the larger the increase in P, the better the improvements of the interpretation.

(On Kendall's Coefficient of Concordance a high degree of relationship between the three judges' ratings was shown. For the difference in their generalization score between No Drug-Chlorpromazine, p is less than 0.01 and is less than 0.02 for the score difference between No Drug and Sodium amytal.)

Relevance Scale

Using Kendall's tau, no relationship was found between the predicted order based on pause/word ratio and the order obtained from the judges' combined ratings (tau = $- 0.200$; signif. $= p = 0.4210$).

Results

The quality of the cognitive solution, i.e. of the level of generalizing from the particular to the universal by extracting meaning from concrete events, is thereby shown to be linked to increase or decrease in pausing—at least in the same individual, under Chlorpromazine. This is not necessarily so under all drug conditions. Under Sodium amytal (S.A.), for example, this link between generating information and hesitation of utterance, between intellectual function and time, appeared to be disrupted—and time rendered sterile. While with Chlorpromazine when capacity for delay was enhanced, intellectual function was too. But where speech action was not delayed, intellectual function was the worse for it.

In all this the question of individual differences must not be overlooked. We have seen that the increase or decrease of P was linked to intellectual achievement (as assessed by judges) in the same person. On the criterion of brevity, we also found that those subjects with longer P habits were consistently more concise.

Common Value

Does this mean that there is a common value to time of planning? That the time of delay is a coin to be exchanged for cognitive achievement?

We have seen that more time meant economy of verbal expression, better style, greater elegance and conciseness. On the other hand, there were individual differences and characteristic ranges of P; individuals were consistent in their tendency to hesitate or utter speech fluently. We must therefore assume something like a characteristic disposition to pausing. (Ramsay (1966), for example, found that pausing habits discriminate between extraverts and introverts; the latter, according to Eysenck's definition (1960) of introversion as the more thoughtful type, were also the more hesitant ones in speech.)

Pause time seems therefore to be composed of two kinds of time; the pause time which an individual is characteristically inclined to invest when generating spontaneous speech at a normal conversational level, and the extra pause time elicited when speech involves more complex cognitive activity. So that if the former is P_{Ind}, and the latter $P_{\text{C(ognitive)}}$, $P = P_{\text{Ind}} + P_{\text{C}}$.

If we take it that Descriptions and conversational speech entail, on the average, a similar level of cognitive effort, and this assumption is supported by the fact that the mean pause time when describing cartoons was not much different from interview pause time, i.e. when no extra intellectual effort is involved, we can substitute for $P_{\text{Ind}} = P_{\text{Description}}$; and if Interpretations entail exceptional cognitive effort, then $P_{\text{Interpretations}} = P_{\text{Descriptions}} + P_{\text{Cognitive process}}$.

We argued therefore that it must be the $P_{\text{Cognitive}}$ which would be commensurate with the quality of Interpretations as assessed by the judges. We therefore subtract P_{D} from P_{I} (to get P), and indeed P_{C} ($=P$) proved then the effective measure (significant at $p = 0.019$) of the intellectual quality of the interpretations of cartoons as between individuals. The larger the P_{Cog}, the higher were the subjects' quality scores. In other words, the effective differential—the common coin of pause time, is the *extra* time invested in cognitive effort over and above the individual's characteristic P, i.e. P_{Ind} as it manifests itself in normal conversational speech. *Taking an individual's inclination towards or away from external activity or his disposition for peripheral versus central processes as a baseline, it seems that the additional time of pausing determines the intellectual quality of the verbal statements.*

Summary to Chapter 4

This chapter deals with the following questions:

(1) How is the global semantic complexity of describing and interpreting cartoons, shown to be reflected in pause length, related to the information content of the component words?

(2) How are specific aspects of semantic complexity such as conciseness of expression and level of generalization reflected in hesitation pauses?

The answer to question (1) was that words used in describing events were easier to predict than those used when interpreting their meaning. Speakers took about the same time to organize themselves to the point of starting descriptive utterances of an average length of 55·8 words as they did to begin interpretations of an average length of 16 words. Thus lexical choice becomes more difficult as the complexity of the semantic process increases. When this was the case, speakers' choices were more individual even where they were more fluent (which might occur after semantic decision had been made). At the level of recoding, information seemed more private and subjective and the communality of the sequence reduced. (2) Conciseness of formulations was shown to be a function of hesitation time spent on it where conciseness was desirable, i.e. in the cartoon interpretations. No such relation was evident in descriptive speech in which conciseness was not aspired. Pausing was shown to be similarly instrumental in affecting the degree and the universality of generalization in the cartoon interpretations. Individual differences pointed to a factor of characteristic disposition to pausing, but extra time invested over and above the individual's characteristic pausing time seems to determine the intellectual quality of verbal statements as between individuals.

Chapter 5

The Cognitive Status of Syntactic Operations

So far we have seen from the evidence shown that the following psycholinguistic processes require a delay of speech action:

(1) the choosing of words,
(2) the recoding of a story, deducing from it a general proposition,
(3) the concise formulation of such general propositions, and
(4) the quality of thought content as judged by level and scope of generalization attained, i.e. the scope of its universal application.

These are semantic processes, of which (1) is also lexical, while (3) and (4) are aspects of the act of recoding.

This leaves us with the syntactic processes, and with the question whether the structuring of sentences can also be classed as a cognitive operation requiring time; if this is so, sentences with a more complex structure should be uttered with more hesitation than sentences whose structure is simple.

The measure used to indicate complexity of sentence structure was the proportion of subordinate clauses in the total number of clauses, a percentage which will be called Subordination Index (*S.I.*). Clause was defined as Subject plus Predicate.

The Subordination Index is a coarse reflection of the degree of hierarchical dependence in sentences, i.e. of sentence structure. For instance, all subordinate clauses were treated as equally dependent, and the structural levels of second, third or fourth order subordination were neglected. These are not entirely neglected though, considering that the proportion of subordinate clauses is by necessity also a measure of the degree of hierarchy, the degree of embeddedness increasing with the proportion of subordinate clauses.

Experiment 1

The data came from two experiments in which three types of spontaneous speech were investigated, the spontaneous description of *The New Yorker* cartoons, the interpretation of their meaning (as described in previous work) and speech uttered during interviews which covered a wide range of topics from objective to subjective connotation. The

Subordination Index (i.e. the proportion of subordinate clauses) was: 19·1% for descriptions of cartoons, 49·8% for their interpretations and 48·5% for interviews. Describing the events in the cartoon pictures seems, judging by these figures, to require considerably simpler sentences than the other two types of speech, i.e. interpretations and interviews.

The difference in simplicity of sentence structure between the descriptions and interpretations coincides with their difference in hesitancy, viz. in the amount of pausing that accompanies them; pausing in the cartoon interpretations—as measured by a ratio of pause time to words produced (P/W) was about twice that in descriptions (Goldman-Eisler, 1961d). If no other speech samples were available we might conclude that the structuring of sentences is yet another cognitive act; that as such it was making its own contribution to the increased hesitancy of the cartoon interpretations as compared with descriptions. One would assume that this would be in addition to the difference due to the cognitive act of interpreting the meaning of the cartoons, such as was shown to be the case for lexical choices (see Chapter 4). However, the fact that speech in interviews was shown to be of the same complexity, with practically the same Subordination Index (48·5%) as the cartoon interpretations (49·8%) calls for further examination especially in view of the fact that pausing in interviews is shorter even than that in descriptions. Pause time per word produced (P/W) in interviews with this particular sample was 0·123 sec; in descriptions 0·166; and in interpretations, 0·340; so that the high Subordination Index in interviews seems achieved without any increase in pause time and we must, therefore, conclude that complexity of sentences and pausing are independent of each other.

Let us consider further circumstances appertaining to the various speech situations. The difference between interviews and cartoon interpretations is that in the latter, speech (content as well as form) is created anew, and the descriptions and interpretations of the meaning of the cartoons have in common the aspect of novelty of speech production. Their content as well as their verbal expression is conceived and verbalized for the first time in response to a hitherto unknown stimulus, the cartoons. They differ, however, in the level and complexity of the conceptual and verbal task they impose, descriptions involving the encoding of visual information in the same order in which it was received, while the interpretation of this information involves processes of abstraction and generalization.

The speech produced in the interviews (in which all kinds of topics, intellectual and personal, objective and emotional are discussed) differs from both the above situations in that in the cartoon test the subject is (a) involved in a creative effort and (b) directed to devote himself to one special operation, whereas interviews allow for a great variety of conditions of speech production, a mixed bag of operations. As in all conversation, automatic verbalization of well-learned sequences will alternate with creative utterance of words and expressions individually selected and fitted to the occasion, and with the new formulation of general content. The properties of each type of speech and level of speech planning must obviously vary, but conversational speech generally involves considerably fewer choices than the speech elicited in response to the novel task of interpreting cartoons.

Such largely habitual verbal behaviour is, as we see from the Subordination Index in interviews, not incompatible with grammatical complexity, and it can assume the form of complex sentences while speech is fluent and pausing minimal.

From this fact it appears that the spontaneous generation of grammatically complex sentences in itself does not require delay of speech action. At the same time semantic complexity when formulating speech anew, in our case represented by the two different speech acts of describing cartoons and interpreting their meaning, has been found to be a strong determinant of the complexity of sentences. Since, as we said before, it also affects the hesitancy of speech, we get a coincidence of pause length and Subordination Index distinguishing the speech situations of description and interpretation. In the light of our interview results, however, this proves to be a spurious correlation.

The significance of the speech situation and the cognitive level for the hierarchial structure of sentences was further illuminated when the Subordination Index was calculated for the same speech situations under drug, that is under Chlorpromazine, Sodium amytal and Amphetamine. The latter two were administered as controls comparing the action of Chlorpromazine with the sedating and hypnotic effect of Sodium amytal and the stimulating effect of Amphetamine.

The important role that falls to Chlorpromazine in the study of the nervous mechanisms underlying linguistic and cognitive (psycholinguistic) changes comes from its widely studied and well substantiated effects on the nervous system and certain aspects of behaviour. Chlorpromazine (Largactil) was the first of the ataractic phenothiazine drugs to be synthesized in an endeavour to discover a drug with a pronounced central depressant action. It is a tranquillizer in the sense that it calms and quietens a patient and it is implicit in this meaning that it does not produce any clouding of consciousness or diminution of awareness—as do sedatives and hypnotics. It is classified as an ataractic drug in the sense that it is capable of diminishing or abolishing mental confusion, delusions or hallucinations. These effects made it into a widely applied therapeutic agent in schizophrenia.

Its relevance in the present context arises from the pharmacological action of Chlorpromazine on the nervous system. It has been shown to depress the reticular activating system thus diminishing alertness and reducing vigilance. At the same time it is claimed that unlike the barbiturates (e.g. Sodium amytal) Chlorpromazine does not depress the Neocortex which is the main part of the brain concerned with the discriminative processes of consciousness, and thus does not interfere with the highest intellectual functions. Delay *et al.* (1959) for instance concluded from his test results, "that Chlorpromazine respects intellectual functions while altering on the one hand elementary psycho-physiological functions, and on the other initiative ('l'allant') and drive ('la spontanéité pulsionelle')". These conclusions and others on this question were however tentative, mainly because little is learned unless the mechanisms by which tranquillizing can release higher nervous activity for effective intellectual functioning are more specifically understood.

The conventional way of measuring cognitive activity by results gives no account of the process by which such results are obtained. It is only by isolating the process or the activities concerned with achieving the results, measuring them separately and treating the respective data in their own right, that drug action might be analysed in relation to the mechanism involved in cognitive activity apart from what it achieves.

Such separation has been made possible by studying the effects of Chlorpromazine and Sodium amytal on hesitation pauses, which, under normal conditions, were shown to be instrumental in cognitive achievement.

The results of these studies suggest that hesitation pauses remain instrumental in cognitive achievement under Chlorpromazine but not under the sedative (Sodium amytal). This was the case in spite of the selective action of Chlorpromazine on pausing, reducing pause time in some subjects and increasing it in others. The intellectual quality of the linguistic product (interpretation of cartoons) as assessed by independent judges (Goldman-Eisler *et al.*, 1965) was found to be reduced as pauses were reduced, and increased as pauses were. This seems to tally with Delay's conclusion that Chlorpromazine affected "l'allant" and "la spontanéité pulsionelle" and not intellectual function directly, but adds the information that indirectly intellect was being affected through the action of Chlorpromazine one way or the other.

The effect of Chlorpromazine (CPZ) on intellectual function was found to be tied to its effect on hesitation pauses, i.e. on its capacity to delay speech action. This indicates that cognitive achievement, of high order at least, depends for its optimum time function on a favourable state of the organism such as may be induced by Chlorpromazine, but also may not, in accordance with individual disposition. From what is known about this drug, this state is part of the tonic condition of arousal or vigilance. The direction of the change induced in it as a result of Chlorpromazine action was found (Goldman-Eisler et al., 1966) to be related to the resting breath rate (RBR) of individuals. RBR was furthermore shown (Skarbek, 1967) to be a disposition of remarkable constancy in individuals. Its level in mental patients was found to be significantly higher than in normal adult subjects, and its decrease to be a reliable indicator of clinical improvement of mental patients as assessed independently by the psychiatrists in charge. As improvement in a clinical sense may be looked upon as the result of a reduction of tension, it is reasonable to see in the resting breath rate a behavioural manifestation of an "initial tension state" as understood by Anokhin (1960).[3]

If Chlorpromazine influenced intellectual function indirectly by way of its selective effect on a mechanism involved in cognitive activity such as manifests itself in the extralinguistic behaviour of pausing, what were we to expect from its effect on such linguistic phenomena as the complexity of sentences? How far would the effect of this drug in depressing arousal and reducing vigilance be reflected in the embeddedness of clauses? This question is relevant because embeddedness may be thought to involve the deferment of the utterance of linguistic elements held in suspense by virtue of an initial "set" in the sense of Lashley's determination of serial order. The increase of "serial ordering", i.e. of the temporal integration or ordering in succession when clauses or phrases are to be embedded in each other, should entail a commensurately increased state of tension between excitatory and inhibitory processes. This would follow if Lashley's contention holds that words or phrases in a state of "partial excitation" are held in check by the requirements of grammatical structure, ready to activate the final common path.

Our facts are incorporated in Fig. 15 and this shows that, in the interview situation, there was a clear and significant drop in sentence complexity (from 52% in the No Drug conditions to 43% under Chlorpromazine with no such change appearing under Sodium amytal).

There were 10 subjects. This change is shared by two schizophrenic patients who received Chlorpromazine (150 mg) orally. The dosage for normal subjects was 25 mg intravenously. A further experiment in which 7 subjects were interviewed under No Drug, Amphetamine [4] 10 mg orally, and Chlorpromazine 100 mg and 150 mg orally, shows the same trend—the figures for the Subordination Index being: 51·2% under No Drug, 50·5% under Amphetamine, and a drop to 46·8% and 44·5% under the two dosages of Chlorpromazine.

In the interpretations of cartoons which showed about the same degree of sentence complexity as the interviews under normal conditions, the effect of Chlorpromazine becomes selective, with the majority of subjects going in the opposite direction to that in interviews and this selective action appears even in the case of the two schizophrenics (a chance occurrence, of course, in such a small number).

This inconsistent and largely opposite reaction of the Subordination Index in the cartoon interpretations is a warning that the changes due to drugs do not affect syntactical processes equally under all conditions. Apart from the nature of the task itself, which is the most powerful

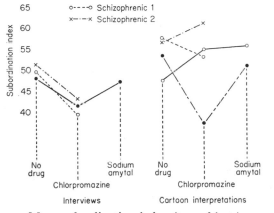

FIG. 15 ●————● = Mean subordination index (ten subjects); ○————○ = mean subordination index (seven subjects); ●—·—·—·—● = mean subordination index (three subjects).

single determinant of sentence structure as the difference between the Subordination Index of 19·1 % for descriptions and 49·8 % in the interpretations shows, a further determinant is indicated. The event of the different effect of Chlorpromazine on interviews and cartoon interpretations, both of which exhibited the same degree of sentence complexity, points to a determinant which may balance and outweigh the effect of Chlorpromazine.

At the relatively more automatic level of speech under interview conditions, the reduction of the Subordination Index under Chlorpromazine might reflect a reduction in the capacity for "serial ordering" which one might assume to support embeddedness of sentences and planning; it also appears that some individuals when challenged to perform at a higher level, as is the case in cartoon interpretations, are able to mobilize defences (probably tonic) correcting for the relaxing effect of the drug. The higher, or unchanged, Subordination Indices of the sentences in the cartoon interpretations of 13 out of our 17 subjects (including the Amphetamine data) would then be the result of a self-regulatory adjustment or overadjustment (in the cybernetic sense) of the organism. This would correct for the heightened relaxation manifest in the less demanding interview situation, by making a compensatory effort. In the cartoon interpretations, the dramatic decrease of the Subordination Index under Chlorpromazine in the minority of cases may be a sign that these individuals were unable to make this adjustment. The structuring of sentences, therefore, does seem to be dependent on a general "set" of the nervous system. This "set" one would assume to be directed towards temporal integration or ordering elements in succession in the Lashley sense which is necessary for the exercise of skills.

As the construction of sentences has so far appeared to be independent of pause time in contrast to word choice and interpretation of meaning, it seems that there are two distinct levels of verbal behaviour. Syntactical operations which profit from the organism's state of efficiency (presumably a tonic state) seem to be organized at the level of skills. Lexical choices, as well as the semantic complexity of intellectual content on the other hand, are functions of the capacity of organisms for delaying speech action. They profit from the time gained in such delays, and this mechanism indicates that they are organized at the level of acts of cognitive creation.

This conclusion is supported by the following further evidence.

Experiment 2

Three sources of spoken language were available:

    (a) conversations and spontaneous talks on selected subjects,
    (b) readings in English and French and
    (c) translations of these texts produced under conditions usual in simultaneous conference interpretations.

The subjects—professional conference interpreters—were placed in a sound-proofed recording booth and the source material was fed to them through ear-phones which were connected to a tape recorder playing back the text to be translated. This was also, and at the same time, fed into one channel of a double-channel Ampex tape recorder, the other channel being connected to the microphone through which the translation of the source text was being recorded.

The tape containing the simultaneous recordings of text and translation is then connected through a Recorded Signal Detector (see Appendix II) to a pen recorder which transforms the sound into a visual record (as previously described). By putting the words to the visual sound traces of the source text as well as of the translation, a record is obtained which shows the sequence between text and translation, and on which the length of intervals, of lag and relative distribution in time can be measured (for example of record see Appendix II).

Such records contain information relevant to various problems but here we are concerned with the specific question of the level of nervous activity involved in structuring sentences and what we can learn about it from the delays and hesitations occurring in the course of their generation. The advantages of studying these in the oral translation performed simultaneously with the reception of the text, as well as in the text itself, is this: the original speaker when generating the source text—this relates to the spontaneously produced texts—operates in three areas of language production; the semantic and lexical as well as the syntactical. He generates content and meaning as well as words and the structure of sentences.

The translator's task is to transform the verbal expression while maintaining the content, i.e. to transform it into as faithful a version as he can manage. He is under total semantic constraint in the area of content and meaning. As he operates under conditions of considerable stress which are inherent in the situation of simultaneous translation, he has priorities to observe. He must not lose the thread of the source text—in other words there are certain limits set by his immediate memory span to the lag he may permit himself—and he must transpose the content of the original passage. If the task is to translate faithfully, as distinct from an assignment to summarize, to make a resumé, he is relieved of content decisions and his lexical and syntactic decisions are free only within the given limits of the text and its content. They therefore become less semantically contaminated, but more pure culture lexical or syntactical. This is at least the postulate of faithful translation, although of course a semantic residue must always be expected.

Concerning syntax, translators have three kinds of choice: they can accept the sentence as structured in the source text simple or complex, they can simplify the sentence structure, or they can produce a more complex structure.

These situations give us three conditions of syntactical activity:

(1) When the source text is generated. Here, sentences are constructed while content is being generated, the situation is one of great fluidity and the syntactical, lexical and content decisions may be assumed to interact.

(2) When the translator sticks to the construction of the source sentence, transposing it from one language to another. Here no decision concerning the kind of construction arises; our question concerning

whether transposing a simple structure is easier than a complex one, may be answered from material uncontaminated by other than syntactical decisions. Although even competent conference translators are occasionally bothered with lexical decisions, the association between source word and translation word is largely an automatic process (it becomes less so if texts are technical or esoteric and the interpreter is unacquainted with their special background. The texts used in these experiments were, however, not of this kind.)

(3) When the translator changes the structure of the source sentence, in which case his decision may be either to simplify or to complicate the source sentence.

To gauge the cognitive status of these activities, pausing under each condition (the measure was a ratio of pausing time to time of speaking $= P/S$) was related to the Subordination Index of sentences taken from 15 texts, 4 source texts and 11 translations. There were 142 sentences, about 9–10 sentences per text. *No relation between P/S and S.I. was found in any of the 15 texts.*

Hesitation in speech (P/S) and the structure of sentences $(S.I.)$ seem two independent parameters of speech whether this was uttered spontaneously by a speaker generating his own content, or by a translator transposing this into another language.

In the translations, in most cases the sentence structure was left unchanged, but where changes of the original structure did occur there was a significant increase (t-test $p=0.001$) in hesitation, whether complex sentences were translated into more simple structures or vice versa. The simplification of complex sentences was in fact a far more frequent kind of deviation from the original structure than complicating simple sentences. Of texts which were relatively simple (with only 10% of sentences having an $S.I.$ of more than 50%), only 17% (5 out of 29) had their sentences constructed differently from the source, with the balance towards simplification. Of texts with a complex structure, when 73% of sentences had $S.I.$s of more than 50%, 44% had their sentences changed (i.e. 18 out of 41) with all but one in the direction of simplification.

In other words, syntactical operations as such, however complex the result, were not reflected in the time of hesitation pauses. Any increase of pause time found was due to cutting loose from the sentence structure of the received input and generating a different one.

(How pausing time between these phases of the process is distributed is an unresolved question. Considering that the second phase, i.e. the independent construction of a sentence, has been shown to be unrelated to pausing, it would seem that the independent syntactic operation in simultaneous translation is delayed by the decision for it as such and by the liberation from imposed constraint rather than by the execution of the fresh course of action, the new sentence structure. This inference, of course, needs to be tested in experiment.)

Conclusion

The above results are in keeping with the previous indication that time is no factor in the construction of complicated sentences. "Set", the state of arousal in the reticular formation, on the other hand, was shown to be so. This illuminates the question of the cognitive status of syntactic operations. Their dependence on reticular activation as shown by the reduction of sentence complexity under Chlorpromazine—together with their independence of the time factor—ranks them in that class of operations which are triggered off by a preparatory attitude. The concentration of selective attention, tonigenic in effect, that goes with it results in a sharply delimited facilitation of the performance of the task in question. We are dealing with the performance of skills, i.e. sequences of most precise movements apparently done with least effort. This minimal effort, however, must have its antecedent in an initial, preparatory effort of concentrating attention, with a neurophysiological representation of tonic stimulation of the activating system. Skills are distinct from plans in that they are subservient to the patterns and rules of the situations set up and initiated by the planning processes. Karl Pribram (1962) writes: "In the case of skills, the regularities in behaviour sequences are sensitive to patterns and schedules of environmental contingencies. In the case of will, however, behavioural regularities cannot be ascribed to the rules, but are attributed to the development by the organism of a variety of intentions or strategies to meet the rules. . . . Interference with intention, or will thus defined, is a function of the anterior frontal engranular and not of the precentral agranular isocortex. . . . The prediction can therefore be ventured and tested that anterior frontal lesions would, and precentral lesions would not affect the . . . distribution of responses in the fixed-interval situation. And such a result would strengthen the body of evidence—obtained from introspection, from ordinary social communication about the problem, and from social and clinical observation and experimentation—that will and skill can be usefully distinguished." It seems that if hesitation is an aspect of volitional action or planned activity then this body of evidence is also in harmony with the distinction which has emerged from our experiments between semantic and lexical operations on the one hand and syntactic ones on the other, when pausing time in spontaneous speech production was the criterion of planning. On this criterion, syntactic operations are to be classed as proficient behaviour, a distinction well in keeping with the guided conformity to rules characteristic of skill as against the initiative of planning and uncertainty of choice which distinguishes volitional action. Thus pauses of hesitation indicate where will or skill operate in the production of speech.

Summary to Chapter 5

The subject of the work reported in this chapter concerns the process of structuring sentences and the question whether this can be classed as a complex cognitive operation. Sentence structure was measured by the proportion of subordinate clauses in utterances. Speech of different degrees of cognitive complexity was studied under normal and under drug conditions, in spontaneous speech and in simultaneous translations.

The spontaneous generation of grammatically complex sentences in itself was found not to require delay of speech action, although the level of cognitive complexity in utterances generally seems to find its reflection in the complexity of sentence structure. Both these factors seemed to interact with the action of neuroleptic drugs such as Chlorpromazine in such a way as to suggest the corrective influence of feedback.

The examination of sentence structure in the light of the concomitant hesitation pauses showing an absence of any relationship between the two indicates that the hierarchical structuring of sentences and embedding of clauses is more a matter of linguistic skill than of planning. Syntactical operations had all the appearance of proficient behaviour as distinct from the volitional aspect of lexical and semantic operations.

Chapter 6

Sequential Temporal Patterns in Speech

So far the measures given of speech in spontaneous discourse were of a uniform entity. The spontaneous speech of the moderately rational person, however, even under the relaxed condition of conversation, may be expected to be a mixture consisting of alternating sequences, some composed at the time of utterance, being novel material, and others consolidated by learning and become verbal habits.

If we assume that planning and organization are intrinsic to the production of speech, and if we take it that hesitation pauses are an index of such cognitive activities, it is not unreasonable to suppose some pattern, some sort of non-random sequential distribution of hesitation pauses.

Experiment 1

Henderson *et al.* investigating this question of pattern in the distribution of pauses (1965), selected several passages of between 350 and 430 continuous words each uttered by one speaker from recorded interviews (5 subjects) as being rational, non-emotional discussions of objective topics, as samples of conversational speech involving cognitive processes. Individual pause and speech periods were measured as usual. At the same time recordings were also made of a passage of prose read aloud (by the same 5 subjects); the successive pause and speech durations were then plotted with speech time along the abscissa and pause time along the ordinate.

When each was fitted overall with a straight line a general speech/pause ratio was revealed which was characteristic for each subject. Within each subject's passage, however, there was an alternating sequence with different speech/pause ratios. Periods with relatively long pauses and short speech utterances alternated with periods with relatively short pauses and long speech utterances.

In fact when lines are fitted to represent the changes in the rate of speech production, we can see a pattern of relatively steep slopes alternating with relatively shallow slopes. This pattern appeared in all samples of spontaneous speech, but not in those of the prose readings.

In this experiment the rate of speech production in readings remained constant (this was not so with further reading samples). Henderson *et al.* argued that if planning goes on in the hesitation pauses, then this alternating pattern might represent a kind of cognitive rhythm, the way cognitive activity advances during speech.

Those periods during which relatively long pauses and short utterances go together (the steep slopes) were assumed to be given over to planning. The supposition was that the succeeding periods of long speech utterances and short pauses represented in the shallower slopes, i.e. the periods of relatively high fluency were the outcome of this planning, and that one might think of the two, the hesitant and the fluent periods, as constituting one unit during the first part of which

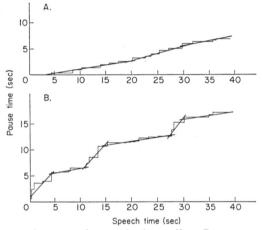

Fig. 16 Temporal patterns in speech. A, reading; B, spontaneous speech.

not only were the semantic including lexical choices made for the local, the concurrent speech, but also for the succeeding periods of high fluency. Or rather, that the speech in these periods of high fluency was the product or the consequence following from the generative activity during the periods of hesitancy. The question then is: if the function of the period of high pausing is one of planning, can the succeeding periods of high fluency be regarded at least in part as a product of this planning? If they are, then the fluency of the speech in the fluent periods (the shallow slopes of Fig. 16), should be reflected in language which is better organized, grammatically as well as vocally.

Therefore the short gaps in the flow of speech which did occur on these shallow slopes were expected to occur at grammatically predictable points mainly (e.g. clause junctures). If the steeper slopes are periods in which the processes of organizing speech were taking place, then orderly phrasing might be expected to suffer. One would expect hesitations in utterances during these periods not to respect the syntactic organization.

To test this hypothesis, the material was analysed with this question in mind with the following results: The preliminary classification of the gaps in the flow of speech as occurring at a syntactic juncture was according to the rules as set out in Chapter 1.

TABLE 13

Gaps occurring during hesitant periods		Gaps occurring during fluent periods	
Grammatical	Non-grammatical	Grammatical	Non-grammatical
61	69	92	58
47%	53%	61%	39%

A chi-square test showed that the hesitant periods contained a significantly higher proportion of gaps which occurred at non-grammatical junctures ($\chi^2 = 5 \cdot 218$, $p < 0 \cdot 025$).

These results show that at the time of uttering fluent speech the speaker's pausing is under control and that it is relatively well integrated into the syntactic structure, that pauses serve the function of communication rather than being symptomatic of internal processes. They are, however, not yet evidence that there is a dependency relationship between the high pausing and the high fluency periods such that together they may be regarded as a unit.

It was therefore argued that if planning occurs in the high pausing period, i.e. on the steeper slope and the succeeding high fluency period, the shallower slope is the result of this planning, then this should be shown by (a) the relation between measures of hesitancy in both periods; the longer the speech/pause ratio of a hesitant period, the smaller the speech/pause ratio should be of the succeeding fluent period and (b) by the fact that the longer the total hesitation time during a period of hesitancy (i.e. on steeper slopes), the longer should be the speech time during the succeeding period of fluency.

The relation as predicted under (a) did not reach the required level of significance ($p = 0 \cdot 0677$) but the relation predicted under (b) proved significant at the level of $p = 0 \cdot 0435$ (Henderson et al., 1965).

Experiment 2

A subsequent, more extensive study (Goldman-Eisler, 1967) brought confirmation of the relation between the time of hesitation in the high pausing periods and the speech time during the succeeding period of fluency (the relation predicted under (b)), whilst relation (a) was not confirmed.

The material of this latter study was based on three types of speech situation:

(a) Spontaneous speech elicited in discussions aiming at engaging the speaker's dialectic and intellectual powers and stimulating him into high level reasoning.

(b) Readings in English, French and German of literary and journalistic texts of various sorts.

(c) Translations of both these samples of speech into French, German and English produced orally and simultaneously by professional conference interpreters.

The analysis of the temporal patterns of hesitant and fluent periods now comprises three levels of psycholinguistic complexity:

(a) Spontaneous speech entailing generative activity of lexical-semantic and syntactic description.

(b) Translation entailing generative acts concerned with lexical and syntactic decisions.

(c) Readings of prepared texts entailing none of these decisions, and concerned with the translation from the written to the spoken modalities of language.

(There were 10 samples of spontaneous speech, 12 readings of prepared texts and 38 translations of which 18 were translations of the spontaneous speech samples and 20 of the readings (there were several translators for most of the texts). These samples contained between three and six minutes of speech (500–700 words.)

The overall degree of fluency or hesitancy of these samples is represented as a proportion of pausing time, a percentage $(P\%)$ in respect of their total duration comprising time of speaking plus pausing $(St + Pt)$. The temporal patterning of these speech samples is described in terms of the significance of the relation between the pausing time (Pt) in the hesitant periods (steep slopes) and the time of speaking (St) in the subsequent fluent periods (shallow slopes). I shall refer to it from now on as "rhythm" or "no rhythm"; the speech samples showing such a significant relationship being treated as having "rhythm" and those where no such relationship was evident being regarded as lacking rhythm, having "no rhythm".

From the figures obtained for these categories it emerged that the pattern relationship between fluent and hesitant periods in speech, that this "rhythm", is a function of the overall fluency. Moreover the indication is that there is a fairly clearly defined limit in the relative time taken up by the output of speech sounds, beyond which temporal patterning, the "rhythm", does not seem to appear. A proportion of pausing less than 30% of the total time of utterance seems to preclude conditions favourable to it. As Table 14 shows, speaking time should not be more than about twice the time of pausing to achieve a rhythmic structure in speech output.

TABLE 14

Pause Time

(expressed as a percentage of total time$=P\%$)

		Less than 30%	More than 30%	
Rhythmic structure of speech samples	Rhythm (present)	2	26	28
	No rhythm (absent)	19	13	32
		21	39	60

$\chi^2=17.9, p<0.001$

All speech samples (spontaneous speech (10)) readings (12) and translations (38)) 16 of spontaneous speech, 22 of readings.

At the same time the figures in Table 14 also show that rhythm is not an invariable by-product of longer pause time but rather that this is a necessary condition for rhythm to materialize. Thirteen out of the 32 speech samples which lacked rhythm did contain the proportion of pausing time required for temporal patterning. On the other hand, most speech samples showing "rhythm" included more than 30% of pausing time, and most of those which included less than 30% showed "no rhythm". This condition prevails whoever the speaker and whatever the context. Only with sufficient time for pausing available, it seems, can speech be organized in units of slow-fast periods of speech production. This is consistent with our general tenet that hesitation is the behavioural concomitant of cognitive activity. The condition for the appearance of "rhythm" in speech as specified above seems to add further support to the conception of cognitive speech as of alternating periods of planning and achievement forming functional units. The ebb and flow of the speech output would then indicate that the cognitive activity during speech has a rhythmic property, and that delay paves the way for verbal activity in a regulated manner in which time has value and a rate of exchange.

That this rhythmic property is functionally meaningful and is the prerogative of cognitive speech is, however, still an assumption to be confirmed; one might infer it, for instance, if (a) the previous finding, that the speech/silence ratio of readings was relatively constant and showing no alteration between periods of hesitation and fluency, were to be confirmed and if (b) the spontaneous cognitive speech (i.e. the spontaneous speech of a certain hesitancy (more than 30% of pausing)) was similarly distinguished from its translations—the latter being transpositions and not original generation of content.

Cognitive Rhythm in Reading and Translating

The relevant values for the readings of prepared texts in the new material show, however, that readings can also be organized in rhythmic patterns of alternating hesitant and fluent periods, and that the selective factor is again that of relative pause time $(P\%)$, the pattern showing itself only when pausing has reached a proportion of 30% or more of the total utterance time.

TABLE 15

| | Pause time Percentage $(P\%)$ | | |
	Less than 30%	More than 30%	Readings
Rhythm	0	3	3
No rhythm	6	3	9
	6	6	12

Simultaneous translations of spontaneous speech, or of readings (see Table 16), present the same picture as is evident from Table 15.

Conclusion and Discussion

It is clear from these results that the rhythmic property in speech suggested to be due to cognitive activity is not the prerogative of spontaneous speech in an intellectually challenging situation as originally assumed. It is also found in an entirely non-spontaneous form of speech output, such as reading, subject to the same condition required for a "rhythm" to emerge in spontaneous speech, namely that a sufficient (i.e. at least 30%) proportion of the total utterance time be given over to hesitation and delay of speech action.

In view of these facts, can we still maintain the hypothesis that the temporal pattern observed is a manifestation of a cycle of acts of planning and verbal production forming a psycholinguistic unit in generative speech? Such a hypothesis would still be reasonable if a case can be made out that the reading of prepared texts, given time, can be a more creative, a more thoughtful activity than was assumed in the first place. What the data showed was that neither the person of the reader nor the text were by themselves decisive factors for the rhythm of the reading, but that what was crucial was the degree of fluency ($P\%$). The same texts read by different readers at different speeds, the same reader changing his speed when reading the same text, showed a difference in respect of rhythm according to the changes in $P\%$.

If one were to think of cognitive speech as the unfolding of an argument, then in the periods of high pausing we would be getting the assembling of the evidence, and in the periods of fluency the winding-up or conclusion. In the case of a reading where this phenomenon is also evident, however, the generator of the vocal product is not the generator of the text of the argument, as in spontaneous speech, and this poses the question of the origin of his rhythm.

As rhythm has also a place in readings one would think that it is an aspect of the text. At the same time, as our various data show, it is also an aspect of the way this is read, in particular of the speech/silence ratio afforded the text. This would mean that, given time, the rhythm inherent in a text can be brought out by a reader. Presumably there must be comprehension—not automatic translation from script to speech. The unfolding of an argument would have to be experienced, to be grasped by the reader, for it to be re-created in the reading performance, in the same way as a musical performer must grasp the musical argument if he aims at interpretation. This then, the interpretation part of reading a text, would involve a reader in cognitive activity of a level outside that which is engaged in the automatic transposition of written into spoken language. This kind of reading was apparently the only one obtained in experiment 1 (Henderson *et al.*, 1965). Basically, however, the rhythm would rest with the text. In spontaneous speech, such texts seem to get generated where speakers take their time—though time taken does not necessarily generate such texts. In reading, such texts would require time to be done justice to or to be re-created. *Time then means opportunity for the reader as well as the spontaneous speaker.*

Simultaneous Translation and Cognitive Rhythm

One of the problems widely discussed among professional conference interpreters is that of the speed of input, i.e. of the text to be translated which is, in the conventional set up, transmitted to the translator through ear-phones. It is held that a rate of input of 150 words/min should not be superceded and that a capacity of translating input up to this speed is attained at the end of training professional conference interpreters (Seleskovitch, 1965). In view of the fact that the rate of speech is predominantly a function of pause time, an increase of speech output per time unit means that less time is left for pausing—that there is more sound and less silence. This intermittent silence between chunks of speech is, however, a very valuable commodity for the simultaneous translator; for the more of his own output he can crowd into his source's pauses, the more time he has to listen without interference from his own output. The disturbance this creates is very striking when unprofessional bilinguals perform—though the professional has his ways of dealing with this situation. Professional interpreters show great indi-vidual differences in mastering this problem. The freedom of simultane-ous interpreters for adjustment is constrained within the fixed limits of the overall time of the particular input to be translated, and while this has not yet been studied systematically, all indication points to a personality factor. The simultaneous interpreter's output cannot last longer or less than that of the input plus or sometimes minus a few seconds, which is the duration of the time lag an interpreter can afford without losing the thread (it was found not to exceed 10 sec, with two-thirds being less than 5 sec).

Within this fixed total time the interpreter is free to expand the pause time at the cost of the speech time and vice versa, while at the same time giving a full translation; he then crams more speech into the shorter periods—and the way in which interpreters availed themselves of this freedom was very characteristic of the individuals. With some, the amount of time was re-distributed between speech and pausing—the pausing getting longer or shorter—while others follow the original distribution fairly faithfully. In the present context the following ques-tions call for an answer:

(1) What is the effect of the rate of input, i.e. the proportion of pause time in the source text transmitted to the interpreter, on the temporal rhythm of the translator's output?

(2) What is the effect of the different ways of re-distributing the pause to speech proportions of time by the interpreter on the rhythmic properties of his output?

The relevant facts were that the pause time proportion of less than 30% of the total time in the interpreter's output does not admit rhythmic alternation of hesitant and fluent periods, and that the rate of input and the interpreter's rate of output were correlated in spite of the adjustments for increasing or reducing the speech/pause ratios. In other words, there were limits to this adjustment because a faster input must of necessity drive the interpreter to increase his speech/pause ratio while a slower input allows him to relax. As the interpreter's rate of output represents an adjustment of the input rate and is the resultant of the two factors, (1) the input rate and (2) his own re-distribution of the speech and pause time components, the two questions posed aimed at sorting out the contribution of these factors to the emergence of temporal patterns (see Table 16).

TABLE 16

| | Pause time percentage ($P\%$) | | |
	Less than 30%	More than 30%	Translations
Rhythm	0	18	18
No rhythm	10	10	20
	10	28	38

$\chi^2 = 12 \cdot 2$, $p < 0 \cdot 001$

A chi-square test based on 38 translations, 18 of which showed the temporal rhythm and 20 which did not, showed no relation between temporal rhythm and the input rate of the source text.

When, however, temporal rhythm was related to the difference between output and input rate, i.e. the increment or decrement in the pause time percentage resulting from the interpreter's re-distribution of pause and speech time, the relation was found to be highly significant. This test was applied to those texts in which some translators had produced translations with a temporal pattern (with rhythm), and others without. There were 12 such texts and in 11 out of the 12, the translations possessing rhythm belonged to those interpreters who had most extended or least reduced pause time. On the other hand, where there was no increment in pause time over that of the input but only a reduction, no temporal rhythm was evident. This was invariably the case when input was more rapid; with comfortable input rates—40% and over—reduction of pause time still leaves a margin allowing for rhythmic translation. When the degree of adjustment for each interpreter is ranked from greatest extension of pausing time ($P\%$) to greatest reduction, the relationship between extension of the lag in translation and the rhythmic patterning of its flow becomes clearly evident (see Table 17).

TABLE 17

Extension to reduction of pausing time

	Higher ranks	Lower ranks	
Rhythm	13	6	19
No rhythm	2	19	21

$\chi^2 = 14 \cdot 8$, $p < 0 \cdot 001$

It seems therefore that in simultaneous translation, speech is generated in rhythmic cycles of high pausing and high frequency periods when the interpreter is actively concerned with the making of pause time.

D

Conclusion and Discussion

This brings us back to the question of what support we get from the data for the assumption that the rhythmic alternation of hesitant and fluent periods is a matter of the complex cognitive activity of planning.

Here a further fact is of some interest. The pause time proportion of 30% necessary for speech output to become rhythmic is an overall percentage covering pausing in the high pausing and high fluency periods.

Pausing in the former is, by definition, a multiple of the pausing in the latter and one might expect that as far as the contribution of pausing time to "rhythm" is concerned, it is this pausing which is the main determining factor. To test this expectation the pause time percentages were calculated separately for the high pausing and high fluency periods (steep and shallow slopes) and classified for "rhythm" or "no rhythm". Pausing in both of these periods turned out to be related to rhythm; the relation was very highly significant (see Table 18).

TABLE 18

	Pause time percentage on					
	Steep slopes			Shallow slopes		
	Less than 50%	More than 50%		Less than 15%	More than 15%	
Rhythm	1	27	28	7	21	28
No rhythm	15	17	32	27	5	32
	16	44	60	34	26	60
	$\chi^2 = 14 \cdot 3, p < 0 \cdot 001$			$\chi^2 = 21 \cdot 4, p < 0 \cdot 001$		

In other words, it is not only the rate of output in the periods of planning that is relevant to "cognitive rhythm" but also the rate of output in the fluent periods, the periods of achievement as we think. Indeed this relation was the closer one of the two.

It would seem therefore that even the most fluent passages of an output in rhythmic speech are under some kind of inhibitory restraint as compared with the fluent passages of non-rhythmic speech. This may indicate that a negative feedback operates even after speech action has left the phase of planning and entered the executant phase, whereas in the non-rhythmic samples the acceleration is more absolute, the action impulsive and the process seemingly uncontrolled.

A division of voluntary movements suggested by Craik (1947, 1948) distinguished two categories: (1) a ballistic movement when "A brief and predetermined force is exerted on the limb which moves for a time, often greatly exceeding the duration of muscular contraction. . . . Movements that fall into this category cannot themselves be modified, but if for one reason or another this intended goal is not reached, a secondary corrective movement may be employed", and (2) movements of longer duration. These are modified by different impulses. Craik (1947) has pointed out that "in playing musical instruments, typewriting, sending morse, etc., complicated patterns of movement are executed at a rate which would be impossible if they were continuously guided by the value of the misalignment with the inevitable time delay".

If speech action is regarded as another instance of voluntary movement, then the distinction in its degree of fluency in the shallow slopes between passages having temporal rhythm and those without it (see Table 18) seems, in the same way as with voluntary movements generally, to be between a ballistic, uncontrollable and a controlled feedback form of action.

The attribute of cognitive rhythm or its absence in speech seems, therefore, to be a manifestation of a totality of attitude, of a specific neurophysiological set pervading the whole situation.

A stop-go style of progression in speech output, which characterizes even the fluent passages on the shallow slopes, appears as a by-product of cognitive rhythm in speech and a manifestation of behavioural cohesion (Bremer, 1966) and functional unity.

Feedback inhibition plays an important role in the achievement of this unity in behaviour (Eccles, 1966) and in the case of activities such as the planning-execution cycle, this notion of set must include not only the general preparatory attitude, but also a very precise preparation for a given activity, a selective process.

Such a state of functional totality was described by Freeman (1940). His dynamotor theory seems singularly fitting in the context of the phenomena reported in this chapter. Freeman postulates cyclical arrangements of tonic and phasic systems to explain the temporal continuities and co-ordinations of behavioural aggregates. This implies a dual conception of behaviour, the (overt) phasic system employing motion, and the (covert) tonic system sustaining posture position and lasting contact. The former is associated with the great pyramidal tracts, the latter with the extra pyramidal tract. However, since the same muscle groups are involved in both tonic and phasic reactions (Allport, 1955), these are really not distinct entities but one, for all intents and purposes—merely stages of the operation of the same aggregate. The "tonic" reaction represents only a less spatially extended and less intense form of the reaction overtly observed as phasic. A "set", since it is based upon a tonic state, can thus be regarded merely as a partial aspect of the full reaction. It can also outlast the overt movements or phasic stages sustaining the steady contacts or positions which must be maintained between the various phasic portions of the behaviour act. "From this standpoint", Freeman says, "sets are to be regarded as specific patterns of the postural substrata in the process of becoming (or at least supporting) phasic reactions." Postural adjustment antedates and sustains phasic adjustment. Set phenomena are thus considered by Freeman to be ". . . expressions of the limiting effects of proprioceptive tonic aspects of response upon exteroceptive phasic activity". Tonic reaction patterns are more economical in that they are slower in reaching their maximal strength and slower to subside. "Phasic-exteroceptive excitants come and go, but the stream of proprioceptive-tonic impulses is measured and continuous."

The dual aspect of set is also contained in Lashley's description of it as a "preparatory ensemble" with numerous "co-temporal" elements in a complex central peripheral concomitance, in Anokhin's (1961) view of its mechanism as of an "action acceptor" and Bernstein's (1967) as of "future anticipation or extrapolation". Ciofu and Floru (1965), who studied the evolution of cerebral bioelectrical activity (EEG at rest and the biopotentials evoked by intermittent photic stimulation) in the course of the elaboration and fixation of set, understood as an attitude of preparation and orientation, distinguished two phases—a diffuse global and a selective discriminative one of adequate preparation. These, they believe, correspond ". . . to the participation of the neurophysiologic components to different extents: the diffuse non-specific component, expressed by global tonigenic activation and the specific, facilitatory component expressed by calibrating tonigenic 'tuning' of the functional structures only". The state of alertness is gradually replaced by precise anticipation of certain signals and the preparation of certain responses within a limited sphere. The evolution of the electrographic picture obtained by Ciofu and Floru expresses conversion of diffuse activity into selective activity.

If temporal patterning in speech apart from being conditional upon the degree of hesitancy is also a manifestation of a specific neurophysiological and tonigenic set, then, according to the above, both pausing and tonigenic "tuning" in combination would be the factors in the temporal patterning in speech. This would accord with the fact that the relationship between rhythm and pausing is closer for high fluency periods (see Table 18) than for the high pausing periods.

It is in the high fluency passages that the difference between rhythmic and non-rhythmic structure correlates most highly with the amount of pausing.

If the hesitancy retained in these fluent passages reflects feedback-control, its closer association with speech of rhythmic structure suggests that the pausing time in these passages contains a tonic charge. According to Freeman's theory, this would be a residual of the tonic state that persists through the movements and overt phasic reactions and sustains the steady contacts between them. *In speech with a rhythmic structure, the involvement of the organism as a whole would consequently differ from that in non-rhythmic speech; whether planning or executing, where we meet with discourse that shows temporal patterning, speakers seem set at a different tonic key, the key of reflection. In the cycle of varying tempi in such speech, even the allegro is sostenuto. This being so cognitive rhythm seems an apposite description.*

Speculation about the origin of this cognitive rhythm, based on a so far cursory examination of texts and on some measurements of the frequency and duration of high pausing/high fluency cycles, may perhaps most fruitfully follow on lines of physical and semantic determinants.

Physical determinants are suggested by the remarkable constancy in the frequency with which the high pausing/high fluency cycle occurs. This was between 3–6 cycles/min independently of individuals, speech situations or languages; there were no differences between these groups and 93% of the sample of 29 texts shown to have cognitive rhythm had mean frequencies within this range, and 76% between 3 and 5 cycles/min.

Taken individually the frequencies of these cycles (there were 251 cycles altogether) were distributed about a mean frequency of 4·2 cycles/min with a standard deviation of 1·6, showing that the distribution was highly centred. 76·2% instead of the expected 68·3% of the total distribution fell between the range from −1 Sigma to +1 Sigma, i.e. between 2·6 and 5·8 cycles/min, showing the mean values given to be representative of the distribution of individual values. It also shows that a stabilizing influence operates over extended passages balancing the fluctuations in cycle fluency.

This suggests that cognitive rhythm might be subject to two influences: one which stabilizes the frequency of the high pausing/high fluency cycle, and the other which lengthens or shortens individual cycles in accordance with transitory requirements. The stabilizing influence evokes an explanation in terms of physical phenomena and more structural permanent entities underlying the tonic regulation of brain structure. As to the influence towards variation, it is tempting to speculate along semantic lines such as the dialectic or syllogistic cycle of thesis and antithesis, of the opening and winding up of an argument. Cognitive rhythm would then be a compromise between nervous and most likely electrical activity in the brain on the one hand and the requirements of the process of reasoning on the other.

Summary to Chapter 6

In this chapter the dynamics of the temporal aspects of speech are examined. The question is raised whether the concept of spontaneous speech as a dual process of planning and execution does not suggest that the occurrence of hesitation pauses forms some kind of pattern. The evidence obtained from spontaneous speech, readings and simultaneous translations confirmed that the successive speech and silence durations can have a regular structure, periods of considerable hesitancy alternating with periods of fluency in a rhythmic fashion.

The necessary, though not sufficient, condition for the appearance of temporal rhythm was found in a defined minimum proportion of the pausing time in the total speech situation, and in the limitations to fluency in the fluent periods of the hesitation/fluency cycle. Readings and translations as well as spontaneous speech were capable of exhibiting a rhythmic structure when fulfilling this condition. The relationship between hesitant and subsequent fluent periods was such that together they seem to form a psycholinguistic unit. The fact that in speech showing a rhythmic structure periods of high fluency were less fluent than in speech showing no temporal rhythm was interpreted to indicate that in rhythmic speech even the fluent phases are under inhibitory restraint presumably as a result of a negative feedback operating.

This seemed to support the contention that such stop-go temporal patterns reflect the stride of cognitive activity in speech and are a manifestation of a general tonigenic set underlying it.

Chapter 7

Temporal Patterns of Cognitive Activity
and Breath Control in Speech

When pauses were classified according to site of occurrence, speakers uttering fluent speech were found more efficient in placing pauses in conformity with the grammatical requirements, i.e. between structural units than when they hesitated: the pauses in fluent speech were well integrated into the grammatical structure. When speech was hesitant, more pauses occurred at non-grammatical places.

When pauses are placed where they do not cut across the syntactic groupings of words and disrupt the continuity of phrases, when they are inserted at the joints occasioned by the structure of sentences, the speaker may be thought to be in control of the communication process. It is reasonable that a speaker who is in control of the psycholinguistic process should make whatever hesitations his planning requires coincide with the grammatical joints available. A complete fulfilment of this aim is achieved in readings but in spontaneous speech speakers can hardly be in complete control of the psycholinguistic process. Thus even in the fluent periods of the samples investigated, only 61 % of the gaps occurred in grammatical places. That such fulfilment is aspired to, however, is shown by the fact that even in the most hesitant parts, on the steep slopes, 47 % of pauses occurred in grammatical places. The difference in this respect between high pause and high fluency periods (steep and shallow slopes) seems to fall in line with the greater difficulty of cognitive tasks associated with hesitant speech, which we may assume usurps attention away from the aim of well-ordered speech production. When the cognitive task is easy, speech is fluent and attention can be paid to grouping linguistic units in such a way that pausing serves communication. Pausing under such conditions becomes rhetorical in function, part of the signalling aspect of speech (Bühler, 1933), whereas when cognitive activity is intense, pauses become part of the symptomatic aspect of speech. Here again the creative act of generating speech interferes with the proficiency of rhetorical performance.

The question of control by the speaker over the act of speech production raises the problem of its organization, timing and dovetailing.

Using the same data measured up for periods of speech and pausing

95

and for high pausing and high fluency periods (steep and shallow slopes) as before (with the relevant words synchronized with each period of speech), the places where breath had been taken were determined (Henderson *et al.*, 1965).

Locating breath inspirations during speech has been found to be relatively simple and easy provided sound recordings are of such quality that breath intakes are audible. They are then marked on the transcripts of the recorded speech where they occur (Goldman-Eisler, 1955).

The points at which breath was taken were again designated as either grammatical or non-grammatical junctures according to the same criteria as used before (see Chapter 1). Breath intakes were also located in the recordings of readings. When these were compared with spontaneous speech, most pauses in the readings were found to serve the intake of breath, while this was not the case in spontaneous speech.

TABLE 19

	Readings	Spontaneous speech	Total
Non-breath pauses	30 (22·6%)	261 (65·9%)	291
Breath pauses	103 (77·4%)	135 (34·1%)	238
Total no. of pauses	133	396	529

In the readings, the proportion of gaps in speech in which breaths were taken was significantly higher than in spontaneous speech. Table 19 shows the data for 5 subjects. In reading, breaths are taken in 77·4% of pauses whilst in spontaneous speech the figure is 34·1%. This is to be expected as the hesitation pauses geared to generation in spontaneous speech fall away in reading. The χ^2 was 7·33 (for 1 d.f. and $p < 0.01$, $\chi^2 = 6.64$).

Both the readings and the spontaneous speech were examined to identify these pauses. They were grouped as occurring at either grammatical or non-grammatical gaps in speech. For this identification the groups were as before.

The total number of breath intakes classified in this way is shown in Table 20. For the values in this table, $\chi^2 = 36.8$ (for 1 d.f. and $p < 0.001$, $\chi^2 = 10.83$). The proportions are very clearly different. Nevertheless, even in spontaneous speech the gaps where breaths were taken were predominantly at grammatical junctures (68·9%).

TABLE 20

	Readings	Spontaneous speech	Total
Breaths at grammatical junctures	103 (100%)	93 (68·5%)	196
Breaths at non-grammatical junctures	0 (0%)	42 (31·5%)	42
Total	103	135	238

What of the remaining 31·5%: are they scattered randomly throughout speech or do they fit a systematic pattern? The cognitive or generative element in speech might well impose its own constraints which interfere with the syntactic governing of breathing. The question therefore is: does cognitive rhythm in fact influence breathing? The breaths taken during spontaneous speech were classified into those occurring in the high pause periods and those occurring in the high fluency periods.

TABLE 21

	Within steep slopes	Within shallow slopes	Total
Breaths at grammatical junctures	20 (54%)	45 (77·6%)	65
Breaths at non-grammatical junctures	17 (36%)	13 (22·4%)	30
Total	37	58	95

As can be seen from Table 21, the percentage of breaths taken at grammatical junctures during periods of hesitancy or planning, 54%, is lower than the percentage during periods of fluency, 77·6% (χ^2 =4·752; for 1 d.f. and p =0·05, χ^2 3·84). This must, however, be seen in the light of the fact previously reported (p. 83) that a lower proportion of gaps designated as grammatical junctures occurred during the hesitant periods, or the steep slopes. The ratios are shown in Table 22.

When correction was made for the disproportion in the number of grammatical and non-grammatical junctures (using arc sinus trans-formations), the difference in breath occurrence (grammatical or non-grammatical) between slopes proved not significant. Breathing, in other words, does not appear to select non-grammatical places for occurrence independently of hesitation. This would suggest that inhalation during speech is a passive process fitting into given breaks in speech irrespective of whether or not these occur at grammatical junctures, and that the decisive factor in breaking up the linguistic groupings at non-grammatical places is hesitation.

TABLE 22

	Steep slopes	%	Shallow slopes	%
Breaths/grammatical junctures	20/61	32·8	45/92	48·9
Breaths/non-grammatical junctures	17/69	24·6	13/58	22·4

There is, however, good reason to assume that the co-variation of hesitation and breathing pauses was not merely due to convenience but that there is a functional background to it, cognitive activity effecting not only a delay of speech action but also interfering with the orderly integration of breathing into the linguistic process. We would have here another example of behavioural cohesion whereby the tendency of cognitive activity to monopolize the attention available to the system extends to, and results in an inhibition of breathing activity. In the light of what was said before (Chapter 6, Discussion), a well-controlled and organized system set at a certain key of functional unity, may be expected to economize on time by using hesitation pauses also for the intake of breath.

To sum up, we have seen that the intake of breath in speech when subjects were reading was governed by the syntactic structure of language. In addition breaths were taken in 77·4% of all the gaps in readings as against 34·1% in spontaneous speech; i.e. two-thirds of the gaps in spontaneous speech were hesitation pauses whilst the proportion of hesitation pauses in readings was only 22% (Table 19). Clearly discontinuities in reading serve a different function than in spontaneous speech and the pattern is materially changed by the introduction of the generative element in speech. The positioning of breath intake is no longer exclusively governed by the constraints of syntax, particularly where speech is hesitant. *Cognitive processes accompanying speech seem to interfere with the orderly integration of such extralinguistic phenomena as hesitation and breathing into the linguistic process. This behaviour seems to flow from the overall set brought on by the cognitive task. Cognitive activity appears as monopolizing and absorbing the attention available to the system. The cognitive processes seem from this to be out of phase with the motor and peripheral processes of speech utterance and breathing.* Further evidence supporting this conclusion will be dealt with in Chapter 9.

Summary to Chapter 7

Two aspects of spontaneous speech, the cognitive and the syntactic, were examined as potential regulators of the incidence of breathing during speech. During passages of prose read aloud, breaths were taken exclusively at gaps in speech designated as grammatical junctures. During spontaneous speech approximately one-third of the breaths were taken at gaps which could not be so described.

In the sequence of alternating hesitant/fluent periods, hesitant periods had a significantly lower proportion of breaths taken at grammatical junctures than the more fluent passages. This, however, coincided with the greater scarcity of grammatical gaps in hesitant passages. This co-variation of hesitation and breathing pauses was attributed to their common functional background of cognitive activity resulting not only in a delay of speech action but also interfering with the orderly integration into the linguistic process of breathing. This was understood to be an indication of central and peripheral processes being out of phase, and of asynchrony in a system preparing for action.

Chapter 8

The Significance of Breathing in Speech

(a) The Rate of Respiration

If we wish to understand the implications of the facts reported in the previous chapter, it is necessary to examine the nature of breath rate during speech, and to determine what distinguishes it from the rate of breathing in non-speech resting conditions.

Under conditions of resting the act of breathing serves primarily and completely the physiological function of survival. During speech it becomes geared to the secondary function of sound production. The regularity of its rhythm is disturbed by syntactic and cognitive requirements and so is the rate of breathing. This is reduced, in most cases of non-emotional speech at least, by the act of speaking as such and, as follows from what we said before, is particularly so when the accompanying cognitive activity is of a high order. The speech breath rate (SBR) of an individual was shown (Goldman-Eisler et $al.$, 1965) to be quite uncorrelated to and independent of his habitual breath rate, taken under non-speech conditions (r=0·02). The range of the latter (RBR) is given as 14–17/min by Judson and Weaver (Voice Science, 1966) and as 12–20 (or 10–18) in the $Textbook$ of $Physiology$ by Bell, Davidson and Scarborough (1965). Skarbek (1967) found the range for normal adults in the waking state even wider, i.e. between 10 and 22 breaths/min, which gives an average of about 15/min (an average of 16 respirations/min was given by Fulton (1955) as the average rate in resting individuals). Judging from the breath rate during speech the possible range was wider, particularly towards the lower end of distribution, i.e 2-25/min. There is, however, no relationship whatsoever between the two distributions. Both parameters, RBR as well as SBR, were shown to be very consistent characteristics of individuals but no indication can be derived from one kind of BR as to what figure to expect from the other. Changes in SBR were shown to be independent of the variability of non-speech resting breath rate (RBR). This is not unreasonable if we consider that RBR is a matter of the autonomic nervous system regulated by the lower brain centres, while changes of breath rate when speech is in progress (SBR) become subject to regulation by

100

the highest brain centres, by virtue of having lost priority in the system to the task of speech production. During speech, breathing becomes a voluntary process controlled at the cortical level and the changes in *SBR* become a function of the type of speech generated (Goldman-Eisler, 1956); as we have seen, the fluctuations of *SBR* from moment to moment showed themselves to be very sensitive to the generative processes involved at any moment as inferred from the oscillations between hesitation and fluency (see Chapter 7).

PSYCHOLOGICAL SIGNIFICANCE OF BREATH RATE

Experimental evidence, as reviewed by Clausen (1951) and Altschule (1953), and more recently by Christiansen (1965), supports the conclusion that while respiratory effects vary markedly in degree and character, hyperventilation is the common accompaniment of strong emotion and mental disturbance. Studies of the relation of respiration and thinking (Golla, 1921) show a picture of reduced breathing activity and breath holding during moments of attention, delays, or irregular breathing. Psychoanalytic writers have frequently stressed the relation between anxiety and breathing (Fenichel, 1953; Freud, 1936; Harnik, 1930; Kubie, 1948). Further evidence showing that in situations associated with excitement and active tension respiratory rate increases, and that relaxation is accompanied by its decrease, is summarized by Skarbek (1967).

The amount of respiratory activity during speech should therefore be expected to indicate strength of affect as far as it finds expression in speech. Easy and free-flowing affect would manifest itself in ample ventilation, whereas repressed affect, attention, caution and fear would be revealed in inhibited breathing.

The rate of respiration, by telling us how frequently the tidal air has to be restored, informs us about the amount of breathing activity. Although to make this information complete the further datum of the volume of tidal air is required, the rate of respiration has been found to be a relatively efficient measure of ventilation (Altschule, 1953; Ax, 1953) and more significant in discriminating between emotional states than an index of volume composed of rate times amplitude (Ax, 1953). Amplitude alone or the inspiration/expiration ratio were not significant at all.

Further, Haldane and Priestley (1935) found that in spite of variation of rate from 3 to 36/min, the alveolar oxygen percentage remained constant, which indicates that increased and diminished rate of breathing is compensated by a commensurate change in volume. Christiansen (1965), in his extensive study of respiratory behaviour, finds a correlation of -0.50 between breathing rate and amplitude. He states that this negative relationship is probably much more pronounced in the resting condition than elsewhere. These findings indicate the presence of a homeostatic respiratory mechanism by means of which adequate ventilation is achieved and lend support to the contention that the resting breath rate as a measure does not only give us information of an isolated respiratory parameter but is a reflection of a specific two-dimensional basic physiological event (Skarbek, 1967).

(b) Breathing in Speech

Two aspects of breathing activity are relevant to the production of speech:

(a) the rate at which the outflowing current of air escapes or is expelled or reciprocally, the degree of ventilation of speech (i.e. the amount of air escaping through speech) and

(b) the neuromuscular activity controlling the action of the respiratory muscles and thus regulating the rate of escape of the expelled air current.

Speech, which normally draws the energy for vocal production from the air escaping in expiration, represents a wide range of controls covering all degrees of air escape, ranging from the most economic use of the outflowing air under strict muscular control to the quicker escape of air in a state of relaxation. Stetson (1928) claimed to have shown that syllables uttered on one expiratory cycle are coincident with the breath pulses through which the exhaled air is expelled during speech. The investigations reported here (Goldman-Eisler, 1955, 1956a and b) proceeded on the basis of these claims.[5] The output of speech uttered during each expiration was therefore taken to measure the rate of expulsion of speech units.

The assumption made in the terms of the process measured was that the greater the speech output during an outlet of breath, the slower the pace at which the inspiratory muscles pass from a state of contraction to that of relaxation, i.e. at a constant speed of talking. What was to be measured was the gradation in controlling the escaping air when speaking.[6]

MEASURING BREATHING IN SPEECH

In view of the importance of breathing to the production of speech on the one hand, and of the emotional significance of respiratory variations on the other, it was thought desirable (Goldman-Eisler, 1955) to break down the measure of speech rate into constituent measures derived from respiratory behaviour during speech. Measures of breathing activity as deflected in speaking and of verbal production as utilizing the energy of the inhaled breath stream—which will be referred to as speech-breathing measures—promised to be immediately relevant to the changing states of affect and tension during conversations.

Technique. The recording of breathing by the usual apparatus, pneumograph, spirometer etc., is undesirable if the speakers are to remain as uninhibited and spontaneous as is necessary in investigations about natural and spontaneous speech.

The noise produced by speakers when inhaling air can on the other hand be heard quite distinctly provided highly sensitive microphones are used and the observer registering them is practised in distinguishing the characteristic noise of breath inspiration. The occasional nearly noiseless inhalations that may not register can be picked up by a throat microphone applied in parallel and connected to a second channel of the tape. However, the near noiselessness of an inspiration implies shallowness and that a small column of air is inhaled. Its failure to register is therefore of not very serious consequence to the account of ventilation over utterances. The incidence of the inhalations recorded and marked on the verbatim manuscript is the raw material from which the speech breathing data are derived.

The Measures. The basic measures derived from such records are:

(1) the duration of utterances (t),
(2) the number of syllables (or words) contained in them (S),
(3) the number of inspirations (I).

From these are derived:

(a) the breath rate $(I/t) = BR$ (or SBR)
(b) the speech rate $(S/t) = SR$,
(c) the output of speech per breath $(S/I) = ER$,
(d) its reciprocal $(I/S) = V$.

S/I measures the rate of expiration or expulsion of syllables to be referred to as ER, whilst I/S should reflect the proportion of the returned air current per syllable spoken. If we express this as a percentage $(I/S \times 100)$, we can speak of a ventilation percentage or index to be referred to as V.

The rate of speech $S/t = SR$ is the product of breath rate and speech output per breath, i.e. $I/t \times S/I = S/t$. From this formula it follows that there could be an infinite variety of combinations between the two factors I/t (ER) and S/I (SR) possible for any particular rate of speech, the output of speech per expiration decreasing as breath rate increases and vice versa. Each particular rate of speech is a hyperbola, the two sides being breath rate and output of speech per breath. Thus when a person speaks at a rate of, e.g. 300 syllables/min, he may have achieved it by inhaling 10 times and uttering an average of 30 syllables between each inspiration, or 30 times speaking only 10 syllables between each breath, or anything between as well as beyond these figures. Thus the same rate of speech would cover very different physiological and psychological processes operating in the production of it. Expressed as the product of breath rate and output of speech (syllables per breath), *SR* may graphically be represented as the hyperbola the two sides of which are the breath rate and expiration rate (Fig. 17). Speech production can fluctuate along any and all of these parameters and constancy maintained in one of them involves variation in the other two.

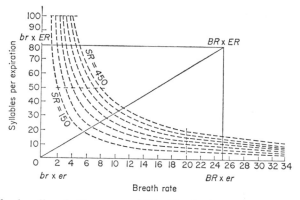

Fɪɢ. 17 The broken lines indicate rates (*SR*) rising by 50 from 150–400 syllables/min achieved at respiration rates up to 34/min and an output of up to 100 syllables per expiration.

Properties and Significance of Speech Breathing Measures. The relationship between the relevant parameters is therefore a dynamic one within a homeostatic system. An utterance described in terms of speech breath rate (*SBR*) and expiration rate (*ER*) in addition to its speech rate (*SR*) is also described dynamically in terms of the neurophysiological processes by which a particular rate of speech output was achieved. With such a relationship one may ask how the actuality of mutual adjustments relates to the potentiality. Whether, for instance, *SBR* and *ER* differ in flexibility or rigidity when it comes to actual behaviour.

Tests of consistency and discriminative capacity of the breath rate in speech (*SBR*) as well as of the expiration rate (*ER*) or its reciprocal *V* showed that not only *SBR* but also *ER* are measures of consistency and capacity of discriminating between individuals, while at the same time sensitive to changes in the speaker's mood during conversations. There were, e.g., significant changes between the first and second (more relaxed) part of interviews (Goldman-Eisler, 1955).

Moreover *V* (*ER*) proved the more reliable as well as more sensitive in discriminating between persons as well as different moods or states of one person. The F ratios in the two comparisons were 11·8 and 29·6 for SBR, and 35·5 and 126·3 for V (ER) and the coefficients of reliability derived from them were 0·957 and 0·983 for SBR and 0·985 and 0·996 for $V(ER)$, all of them significant far beyond $p < 0.001$.

When degrees of constancy and variation were compared for these quantities and for SR, it became evident that speakers adapt to the requirements of situation, topic and interlocutor mainly through variations in the rate of speech output (SR) and that they preserve balance by keeping the economy of air outflow per speech unit (ER) constant (Goldman-Eisler, 1955).

Deviations from the level preferred of ER must therefore be interpreted as being signals of a different, more vital, significance in respect of the speaker's equilibrium than are fluctuations of speech rate. For if we take the fluctuations of breath rate as indications of the ebb and flow of affect strength (or states of excitation) (Goldman-Eisler, 1955), a constant level of ER would indicate that the affect is under sufficient control to be channelized through verbal activity. A deviation from this preferred level would then be an indication that the balance between the forces of affect and control and the processes of excitation and inhibition has been upset. A reduction in the output of syllables per breath means that a larger proportion of the inhaled air current escapes unused as steam from an engine, i.e. emotional excitation has not been channelled through the process of verbalization. High breathing activity with low verbal output shows excitation to be unattached and unmarshalled by speech and all that speech activity involves, such as conceptualization, the symbolic process, or connections of affect with cortical activity. What is measured is the delay in the relaxing phase of the respiratory cycle, while the length of the contraction-relaxation cycle depends on the rate of respiration. The two activities of breathing and speaking are continually interacting and the level of control cannot be judged on the basis of verbal transformation as measured by the expulsion rate (ER) only; the intensity of the excitation as measured by breath rate must also be taken into account. Different levels of respiratory activity set the organism engaged in speech different tasks. To maintain the same rate of speech production, e.g. 200 syllables/ min, at a low breath rate of, say, 4 respirations/min, an output of 50 syllables/breath is required, which taxes the speaker's capacity for gradual release action to quite an extent. To maintain the same speech rate at a breath rate of 20 respirations/min, on the other hand, an output of only 10 syllables/breath is required which is not only easy to accomplish, requiring a lesser degree of voluntary control, but leaves the speaker with a surplus of expiratory air current to play with and use, so as to give his speech expression and rhetorical colour.

This difference is evident from Fig. 17. When the speech rate is changed, the rearrangement in the pattern of speech production may involve changes such as the following: assuming a speaker accelerates to produce 360 syllables/min, a breath rate of 4/min will then hardly be supportable since it would require an output of 90 syllables/breath (though this is not impossible to achieve, see Goldman-Eisler, 1956a). Normally, however, with acceleration of speech the speaker will also accelerate breathing, particularly where its rate has been too low for the requirement of verbal production. A breath rate of 20/min will allow a speaker 18 syllables/breath instead of 10 as before, thus leaving him less margin for expression and rhetoric. If he wants or is impelled to use speech in a more expressive way, he will have to slow down or breathe more often. *In this is implied that expiration rate (ER) and breath rate while being contingent and correlated, measure independent aspects of speech production* (Goldman-Eisler, 1956b).

Summary to Chapter 8

The phenomenon of continuity in speech utterance and its interruptions required an explanation of the gaps in speech due to breathing beside those due to hesitation. In this chapter the nature and significance of breathing during speech is examined and compared with breathing behaviour at rest. The independence of breathing behaviour under these two conditions is linked to the different levels of regulation involved. Two aspects of breathing activity were analyzed to derive objective measures of states of excitation and its control during speech through the recording of continuous and spontaneous speech. Their properties of constancy and variability are described and the psychological significance of changes in these respects discussed.

Chapter 9

Experimental Validation of
Speech-breathing Parameters

Validation of the hypotheses formulated in the last chapter concerning the psychological significance of *SBR* and *ER* was first attempted in the light of a clinical analysis of the content of speech uttered in psychiatric interviews (Goldman-Eisler, 1956a). It was followed by physiological (Goldman-Eisler, 1956b) and psychopharmacological evidence. A factor analysis based on the latter (Goldman-Eisler *et al.*, 1965) and including hesitation behaviour, was then carried out for further elucidation.

(a) Speech Breathing Activity, Content and Muscular Tension in Psychiatric Interviews

The speech output of eight psychiatric patients was grouped either in terms of the topics discussed or, where the content was not sufficiently structured to permit such classification, according to assessments of the emotional significance of utterances made by psychiatrists (see Table 23).

While the universes of the *SBR* and *ER* values differed widely between individuals, as is evident from Fig. 18, each universe was clearly structured in terms of the preferences of *SBR* in respect of emotional intensity and intellectual level. Depending whether the topics discussed or statements made could be classified as of outgoing or restricted affect, and the speech as emotional or intellectual, *SBR* in the emotionally outgoing parts occupied high and *ER* low ranges, whilst in intellectual speech of restricted affect, *SBR* was low and *ER* high.

Out of 124 topics discussed or statements assessed by psychiatrists, 110 were in the expected area of either the first category (47) of high *SBR* and low *ER*, or the second of low *SBR* and high *ER* (63).

Considering the high correlation of the two parameters one may ask whether there was not redundancy in our measures and what the addition of *ER* adds to the information yielded by *SBR*.

What is to be noted in this context, however, is that while *SBR* and
107

TABLE 23

Topics implying free-flowing and out-going affect		No. of statements	Topics implying restricted emotionality, tension states, or intellectual speech	No. of statements
S. I	Wish to be a little boy	3	Information theory	11
	Jealousy	6	Intellectual reaction to art	2
	Reaction to cruelty	2		
S. II	Pleasure through bread and butter	5	Deprivations	7
			Rejection	4
	Compassion for mother	5		
S. III	Sex	3	Mother as inhibiting force	8
	Mother in need of protection	3	Church, Morality	1
	Outcry: "I want to be free!"	1		
S. IV	Aggression against women	6	Aggression against men (which turns into something sweeter)	5
			Reasoning	5
S. V	Hopes and expectations (marriage to protective woman)	4	Money, career	4
			Anxieties (marriage to dominant woman)	4
	Psychotherapy—woman therapist	3		

Psychiatrist's ratings

S. VI	Disturbed, excited, affect	5	Inhibited, thinking, cautious, fear of drowning	4
	Some affect, uncertain	1		
S. VII	Unguarded	2	Guarded	4
	Anxious, milder	1	Anxious, worried	1
S. VIII	Tense (t + +), Non-fear	3	Less Tense (t −)	5
	Tense (t +), Non-fear	5	Tense (t), fear of strangulation and horror of exams	1

S. = Subject.

ER are highly correlated, they are not entirely covariant and independence between these parameters is indeed a possible actuality.

Multiple time series calculated from registered values of *SBR*, *ER*, the action potentials of forearm muscles (*AP*) and speech rates (*SR*) during interviews showed periods of wide divergence of *SBR* and $V (=\frac{1}{ER})$ occurring when *SR* was decreasing and *AP* was starting to rise (Goldman-Eisler, 1956b). Hesitant but highly ventilated speech seems from this to occur without a concurrent rise in *SBR* when the electromyographic measures taken simultaneously show high tonicity in the system.

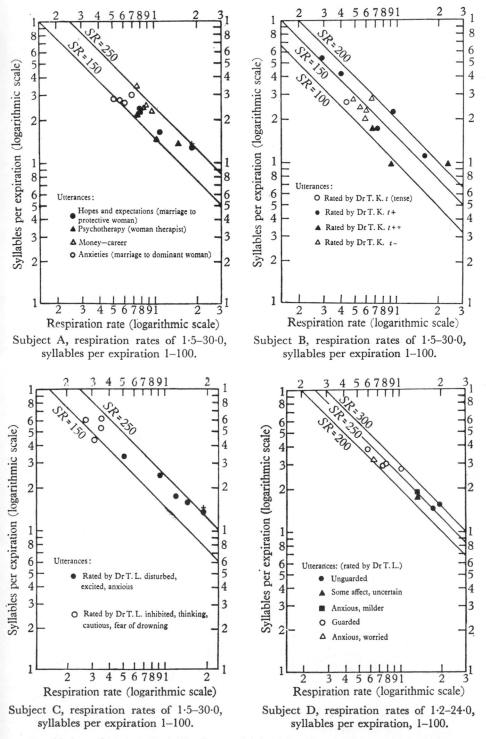

Subject A, respiration rates of 1·5–30·0,
syllables per expiration 1–100.

Subject B, respiration rates of 1·5–30·0,
syllables per expiration 1–100.

Subject C, respiration rates of 1·5–30·0,
syllables per expiration 1–100.

Subject D, respiration rates of 1·2–24·0,
syllables per expiration, 1–100.

FIG. 18 Logarithmic scales indicating respiration rates for 4 subjects and for syllables
per expiration.

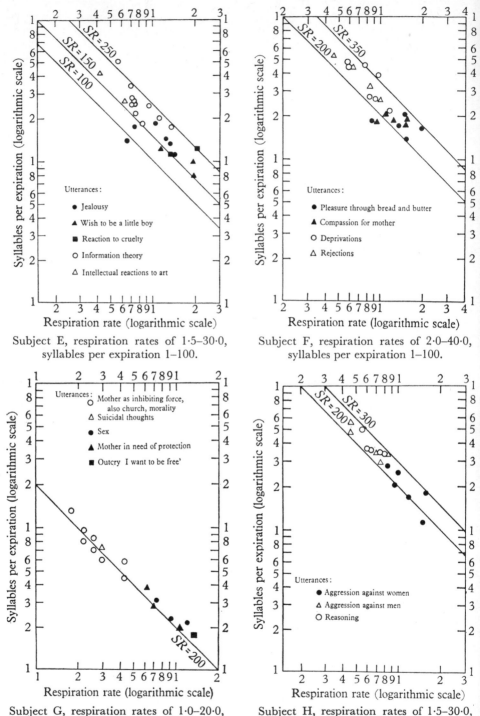

Subject E, respiration rates of 1·5–30·0,
syllables per expiration 1–100.

Subject F, respiration rates of 2·0–40·0,
syllables per expiration 1–100.

Subject G, respiration rates of 1·0–20·0,
syllables per expiration 10–1000.

Subject H, respiration rates of 1·5–30·0,
syllables per expiration 1–100.

Such a period of asynchrony is followed by a relative synchrony of these reactions (Fig. 19).

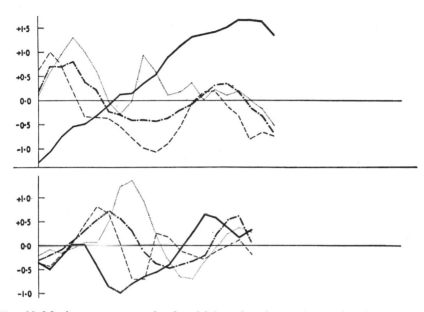

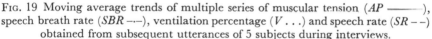

FIG. 19 Moving average trends of multiple series of muscular tension (*AP* ———), speech breath rate (*SBR* –·–), ventilation percentage (*V* . . .) and speech rate (*SR* – –) obtained from subsequent utterances of 5 subjects during interviews.

(b) Speech Breathing Activity and the Effect of Chlorpromazine

If the degree of variation of *ER* relative to the variation of *SBR* reflects the degree of response at the cortical level (by adjusting rate of speech output) to variations at the autonomic level (of breathing activity), then one would expect such response to be reduced under Chlorpromazine in view of the action of this drug of inhibiting the arousal function of the reticular formation, by blocking the access of the arousal stimuli to the cerebral cortex.

Such an effect would show itself in a relatively small rate of change of *ER* compared with the concomitant rate of change of *SBR*. When *SBR* covers a wide range of variation, *ER* should remain relatively constant.

This would manifest iself in the slope (regression line of *ER* on *SBR*) tending toward the horizontal, while a steep slope would indicate a rate of change in ER corresponding to the rate of change in SBR. The following figures may illustrate the possible relationships and their implications.

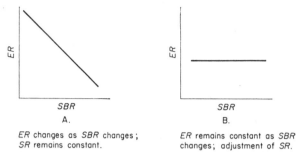

A.

ER changes as SBR changes;
SR remains constant.

B.

ER remains constant as SBR
changes; adjustment of SR.

FIG. 20 A, Expiratory control reflects respiratory activity. B, Expiratory control unaffected by respiratory activity.

THE EXPERIMENT

Ten subjects were interviewed for about 30 min under 3 conditions: (1) Normal (No Drug); (2) Chlorpromazine (25 mg intravenous); (3) Sodium amytal (300 gr intravenous) (Goldman-Eisler et al., 1967). The interviews were transcribed and 15 periods of continuous speech lasting 1 min were measured to obtain the number of breath intakes and number of words produced. The breath rates and expiration rates for each minute's conversation were calculated for each condition and the slopes between SBR and ER were computed.

TABLE 24

Significance of differences between slopes (a) of ER on SBR (based on 15–20 readings each) in three conditions (p = probability level)

			Condition			
	No Drug		Chlorpromazine		Sodium amytal	
Subjects	a	$p(ND\text{-}CPZ)$	a	$p(ND\text{-}SA)$	a	$p(CPZ\text{-}SA)$
lac	− 12·49	0·00009	− 3·27	0·05257	− 1·47	0·16141
iew	− 1·83	0·01782	− 0·86	0·05950	− 2·53	0·00001
eba	− 3·18	0·00027	− 1·17	0·02731	− 2·00	0·05897
neb	− 1·23	0·04833	− 0·72	0·08020	− 1·20	0·11921
lew	− 1·50	0·24285	− 1·28	0·98573	− 1·27	0·35242
nom	− 1·51	0·22388	− 0·80	0·20194	− 2·42	0·09250
log	− 4·89	0·00002	− 2·44	0·12197	− 3·18	0·23348
erg	− 1·48	0·14055	− 0·88	0·21617	− 0·65	0·29383
caj	− 2·50	0·26674	− 1·93	0·13976	− 1·07	0·20645
hoj	− 2·23	0·44915	− 2·39	0·24242	− 1·56	0·15222

RESULTS

Table 24 shows the slopes for each subject and each condition. The difference in the slopes between the conditions for each subject (the mean slopes were: $-3\cdot28$ for No Drug, $-1\cdot59$ for Chlorpromazine and $-1\cdot74$ for Sodium amytal) were subjected to a significance test for slopes (Student's t) based on residuals and under p are entered the probability levels of t for each individual. For all except 1 subject, the rate of change of ER had decreased under Chlorpromazine, in 5 cases significantly and in 3 cases extremely so.

(A further experiment in which six subjects were interviewed under No Drug, Chlorpromazine (100 and 150 mg by mouth) and Amphetamine (10 mg) showed the following mean slopes: No Drug $1\cdot06$ Amphetamine $1\cdot10$, Chlorpromazine 100 mg $0\cdot62$ and Chlorpromazine 150 mg $0\cdot55$). Sodium amytal showed a less pronounced effect. While 8 subjects were similarly affected, the only significant difference was in the opposite direction, the slope being steeper under Sodium amytal than the No Drug as well as Chlorpromazine conditions.

DISCUSSION AND CONCLUSION

Chlorpromazine had the most significant effect where the effort of accommodating the necessary articulatory movements within the expiratory phase was habitually greatest under No Drug conditions, i.e. with individuals whose efficiency of transforming the respiratory energy into a quantity of language was of a high order (with the highest ER). Individuals with a lesser degree of control by the speech centres over the breathing muscles (with the smaller mean ER) seem, as far as maintaining their level of effort is concerned, less vulnerable under the drug, obviously because they operate at a less demanding level to start with, and this is more easily maintained constant through the variations of breath rate.

TABLE 25

Intercorrelations (Spearman Rank correlation coefficients)

	a ND	a CPZ	a SA	ER ND	a ND-CPZ	a ND-SA
a ND						
a CPZ	0·794†					
a SA	0·454	0·103				
ER ND	0·951†	0·733*	0·386			
a ND-CPZ	0·667*	0·545	0·491	0·655*		
a ND-SA	0·745†	0·830†	−0·122	0·376	0·467	

Note. ND= No Drug; CPZ= Chlorpromazine; SA= Sodium amytal.
* $p<0\cdot05$
† $p<0\cdot01$

The regression of ER on SBR in response to the relaxing effect of Chlorpromazine in respect of arousal and the tension state (Anokhin, 1960) of the nervous system lends further support to the interpretation of *ER* as the indicator of the strength of control and of *SBR* as that of the intensity of excitation. Chlorpromazine relaxes the control involved in marshalling respiratory energy to speech production, and this is also consistent with the finding that the arousal function is depressed by Chlorpromazine. This becomes more evident where the initial state of arousal or tension is of a high order. That this is so may be seen from the fact that in spite of the considerable change in slopes between *ER* and *SBR* between no Drug and Chlorpromazine (from -3.28 to -1.59), the rank order of slopes had remained the same as under No Drug condition not only in respect of the slopes themselves ($r=0.794$, $p<0.01$) but in respect of the expiration rate under No Drug conditions ($r=0.733$, $p<0.02$). No such function was found to exist for Sodium amytal. What was lost under this drug was the individual's characteristic response; the rank order resulting from Sodium amytal influence bears no relation whatsoever (0.103) to the normal differences.

RESPIRATION, HESITATION AND PERSONALITY

The relevance of *SBR* to excitation and inhibition, of *ER* to control of excitation and of *P* (i.e. the extra time taken for cognitive work (Henderson *et al.*, 1965)[7] to capacity for delaying speech action, has suggested their relevance to tonicity. The high reliability of *SBR* and *ER* and the power of *P* to sort out individuals as well as the difference of cognitive quality ($p<0.001$) (Henderson *et al.*, 1965) commended these parameters as indicators of the tonic condition or set of the performing organism.

If we view emotional and cognitive processes as manifestations of states of excitation and inhibition, their antagonistic nature seems a reasonable assumption. In Hughlings Jackson's words, ". . . with the fall of the intellectual element there is a rise in the emotional one". The situation when regarded in these terms looks rather more complicated and the simple opposition of the two processes may not be immediately acceptable. It is therefore useful that we have developed and available for testing purposes two parameters of speech which were shown to measure emotional and cognitive processes, namely *SBR* and *P*. If emotion and intellect are antagonistic, one would expect the speech breath rate (*SBR*) to be inversely related to pausing in speech (*P*). This was indeed the case.

The correlation between amount of pausing and frequency of breathing was negative not only when the two parameters were derived from the same material, i.e. when the dependence might have been operational (Goldman Eisler, 1956c) (see Table 26). The inverse relationship between *SBR* and *P* was also maintained when the two parameters were derived from two different situations and levels of verbal plan-

TABLE 26

Correlations between percentage time of pausing $(P\%)$ and
speech breath rates (SBR) for 8 subjects.

SBR	$P\%$
S. I.	$-0\cdot018$
Co.	$-0\cdot225$
He.	$-0\cdot207$
S. II.	$-0\cdot695\ddagger$
Jo.	$-0\cdot352*$
Mu.	$-0\cdot394\dagger$
Pea.	$-0\cdot656\ddagger$
B. I.	$-0\cdot155$

* $P=0\cdot05$
† $P=0\cdot01$
‡ $P=0\ 001$

ning for any one individual, SBR from interviews and P from the
cartoon experiment. Those subjects whose SBR was high in the interviews were consistently pausing less in the cartoon interpretations than
those whose breathing was less frequent $(r = -0\cdot68)$. This points to a
more permanent link characteristic of personality (see Fig. 21).

Table 27 of intercorrelations between measures of pausing and speech-
breathing measures also includes ER and a quantity called RBR-SBR.
This is the differential, in most cases a reduction, between the breath
rate of subjects in a state of rest (RBR) and when speaking (SBR). It is a
measure of the degree of modification of normal breathing due to speaking. Table 27 shows that pausing in hesitation $(P$ and $P/W)$, control of
expiration (ER) and adjustment of breathing activity to speech $(RBR$-
$SBR)$ form a cluster opposite to SBR which was shown to increase with
affect and excitation.

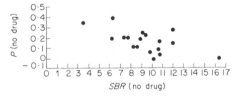

FIG. 21 Relation between breath rate in interviews and pause increment in interpretations of cartoon meanings (generalizations). $P=$ Pause differential; $SBR=$ speech
breath rate.

This syndrome suggests that an individual's habitual degree of controlling or adjusting breathing activity to speech production and his
capacity to delay speech action in response to a complex cognitive task
are manifestations of the same underlying condition. A factor analysis

based on these intercorrelations resulted in a first factor highly saturated with these parameters (see Table 28), and clearly of an inhibitory nature. From its associations, it is reasonable to think of it as a control,

TABLE 27a

Intercorrelations (19 subjects)

	SBR_{ND}	ER_{ND}	RBR_{ND}-SBR_{ND}	P_{CPZ}	P_{ND}	P/W_{ND}	P_{CPZ}-P_{ND}	RBR_{ND}
SBR_{ND}								
ER_{ND}	-0.80							
RBR_{ND}-SBR_{ND}	-0.71	0.65						
P_{CPZ}	-0.60	0.60	0.57					
P_{ND}	-0.51	0.46	0.33	0.64				
P/W_{ND}	-0.33	0.25	0.45	0.21	0.27			
P_{CPZ}-P_{ND}	-0.20	0.21	0.35	0.70	-0.02	0.13		
RBR_{ND}	-0.19	0.27	0.83	0.32	0.06	0.37	0.33	

SBR_{ND} = Speech breath rate under no drug.
ER_{ND} = Expiration rate, i.e. number of words per breath under no drug.
RBR_{ND}-SBR_{ND} = Differential between resting breath rate and speech breath rate both under no drug.
P_{CPZ} = Pause differential under Chlorpromazine.
P_{ND} = Pause differential under no drug.
P/W_{ND} = Pause time per word produced in cartoon interpretations under no drug.
P_{CPZ}-P_{ND} = Change of P under Chlorpromazine.
RBR_{ND} = Resting breath rate under no drug.

inhibition or effort factor of personality, the effort being inferred from the extra pause time P being spent in interpreting cartoons, i.e. when the cognitive operation required was more complex. The inverse relationship of SBR and P is in keeping with the idea of an emotional-cognitive polarity along one continuum. This interpretation was further supported by the fact that SBR proved a function of the amount of reduction or adjustment in an individual's breath rate between the resting rate (RBR) and speech breath rate (SBR) (Goldman-Eisler et al., 1965). When we consider that this differential in the two breath rates $(RBR$-$SBR)$ reflects the degree to which the cortical act of speaking inhibits the more automatic function of breathing, SBR appears as the result of this inhibition. Further corroborating facts are the values of SBR under the different conditions of speech production. The mean SBR derived from spontaneous speech generated in interviews was 12·8, from readings of prepared texts, a relatively automatic speech activity, 16·5, whilst the mean resting breath rate (RBR) of these subjects was 15·8 (Skarbek, 1967). Thus, reading, the more mechanical act of speech production, does not reduce RBR whilst spontaneous speech, i.e. the creative act of speech generation, does (mean RBR-SBR in interviews = 3·05, in readings = -0.07).

TABLE 27b
Intercorrelations (12 Subjects)

	SBR_{ND}	ER_{ND}	RBR_{ND}-SBR_{ND}	P_{ND}	P/W_{ND}	P_{CPZ}	P_{SA}	P_{CPZ}-P_{ND}	RBR_{ND}	P_{SA}-P_{ND}
SBR_{ND}										
ER_{ND}	-0.78									
RBR_{ND}-SBR_{ND}	-0.69	0.52								
P_{ND}	-0.68	0.64	0.48							
P/W_{ND}	-0.68	0.44	0.36	0.74						
P_{CPZ}	-0.60	0.61	0.58	0.70	0.50					
P_{SA}	-0.49	0.25	0.46	0.62	0.49	0.44				
P_{CPZ}-P_{ND}	-0.15	0.30	0.30	0.01	-0.15	0.70	0.01			
RBR_{ND}	-0.02	0.14	0.68	-0.01	-0.34	-0.25	0.16	0.43		
P_{SA}-P_{ND}	0.39	-0.44	-0.26	-0.58	-0.58	-0.38	-0.20	0.11	0.16	

These facts indicate that breathing behaviour as it manifests itself during spontaneous speech, i.e. when the complex cognitive processes of speech generation are in progress, undergoes a degree of modification which makes its reduction an indication of the degree of control and internal inhibition (in Pavlovian terms). As subjects are differentiated

TABLE 28a
Factor loadings

F 1 (49·9% of variance)		F 2 (16·9% of variance)		F 3 (14·0% of variance)	
$RBRS_{ND}$-BR_{ND}	0·889	RBR_{ND}	0·681	P_{CPZ}-P_{ND}	0·704
SBR_{ND}	−0·819	P_{ND}	−0·592	P/W_{ND}	−0·509
P_{CPZ}	0·835	P_{CPZ}-P_{ND}	0·437	P_{CPZ}	0·484
ER_{ND}	0·801	SBR_{ND}	0·349	RBR_{ND}	−0·245
P_{ND}	0·593	ER_{ND}	−0·300	RBR_{ND}-SBR	−0·232
RBR_{ND}	0·589	RBR_{ND}-SBR_{ND}	0·292	SBR_{ND}	0·098
P/W_{ND}	0·498	P/W_{ND}	0·190	ER_{ND}	−0·050
P_{CPZ}-P_{ND}	0·493	P_{CPZ}	−0·110	P_{ND}	−0·047

TABLE 28b
Factor loadings

F 1 (47·4% of variance)		F 2 (21·2% of variance)		F 3 (12·3% of variance)	
SBR_{ND}	−0·878	RBR_{ND}	0·849	P_{SA}	0·778
P_{ND}	0·875	P_{CPZ}-P_{ND}	0·725	P_{SA}-P_{ND}	0·581
P_{CPZ}	0·842	P/W_{ND}	−0·552	P_{CPZ}-P_{ND}	−0·370
ER_{ND}	0·795	P_{SA}-P_{ND}	0·469	ER_{ND}	−0·255
RBR_{ND}-SBR_{ND}	0·755	RBR_{ND}-SBR_{ND}	0·423	P_{CPZ}	−0·194
P/W_{ND}	0·740	P_{ND}	−0·274	RBR_{ND}-SBR_{ND}	0·118
P_{SA}	0·583	P_{CPZ}	0·270	P/W_{ND}	0·115
P_{SA}-P_{ND}	−0·525	SBR_{ND}	0·103	P_{ND}	0·102
P_{CPZ}-P_{ND}	0·298	P_{SA}	0·060	RBR_{ND}	0·067
RBR_{ND}	0·195	ER_{ND}	0·028	SBR_{ND}	−0·059

and characterized by their preferred degree of this modification, we may consider this to be a reflection of their habitual state of intellectual and cortical tension.

In addition to Factor 1, a second Factor was extracted. Factor 2 was saturated with the change of P under the effect of Chlorpromazine (P_{CPZ-ND}) whereby a lengthening of P was accompanied by improvement and a reduction by deterioration of intellectual performance (Goldman-Eisler et al., 1965) and with the resting breath rate (RBR). This factor is orthogonal (see Fig. 22) to the first factor and independent of any tendency in the individual to inhibit or to control speech as measured through P, SBR and ER. It points to a link between the effect of Chlorpromazine on complex cognitive operations and the more basic act of breathing subserving its physiological function primarily.

The association of this effect with *RBR* and the power of this resting but waking breath rate to discriminate between individuals, which *RBR* during sleep does not,[8] suggests a characteristic level of arousal on the lines of Anokhin's "initial tension state". This is further supported by the findings (Skarbek, 1967) that *RBR* is significantly higher in

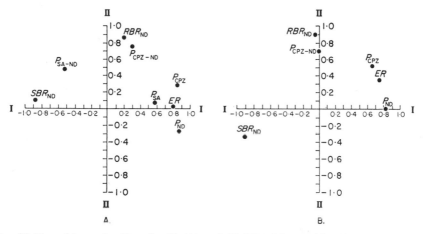

FIG. 22 Plot of factor loadings for 12 (A) and 19 (B) subjects with reference to factor axes I and II. For part (B), the factor loadings were rotated by 45°. *SBR* = Speech breath rate; *P* = pause differential; *ND* = no drug; *RBR* = resting breath rate; *CPZ* = chlorpromazine; *SA* = sodium amytal; *ER* = expiration rate, i.e. number of words per breath.

mental patients than normal subjects and that clinical improvement in the former is accompanied by a decrease in *RBR*. This condition seems therefore a more basic and permanent tension state than the selective set towards cognitive tasks represented in Factor 1. While the role of *RBR* as an indicator of this level of arousal needs further study, certain conclusions may be drawn as to the pattern of processes underlying the production of speech which favour cognitive processes in its generation and the intellectual quality of the resulting product.

The relationship which was thus demonstrated between the two types of gap which interrupt the flow of speech production, one due to hesitation and the other to breathing, enables us to view the duality of language as an external manifestation of the dynamics of two interacting functions of an organism in the act of speech production. The various aspects of this duality in the organism and nervous system, in behaviour, in mental processes and in language are listed below.

ASPECTS OF DUALITY

IN LANGUAGE:

Symbol	Signal
Meaning	Context
Semantic aspects	Grammatical constraints
Content words	Structural words
Long words	Short words
Rare words	Frequent words
Novel words	Predictable words
Information (low transition probabilities)	Redundancy (high transition probabilities)

BEHAVIOUR AND
ITS PHYSIOLOGICAL BASIS

Delay of speech action (pausing)	Speech action (fluency)
Inhibition (low *SBR*)	Excitation (high *SBR*)
Muscular contraction gradually released—high control (high *ER*)	Muscles relaxed, poor control of release (low *ER*)
Alertness	Slackness
Tonic condition (tension)	Relaxed condition
Central activity	Peripheral activity
Voluntary processes	Automatic processes

PSYCHOLOGICAL PHENOMENA

Vigilance (attention)	Nonchalance
Planning	Trial and error
Organizing	Serial ordering
Deliberate thought	Impulsive action
Association by similarity (abstracting—generalizing)	Association by contiguity (conditioned responses and historical connections)
Cognitive activity	Emotional excitement
Choice	Chance (random behaviour)
Recoding	Rote learning
Production	Reproduction
Originality	Cliché

Summary to Chapter 9

The subject of this chapter is the experimental validation of the psychological significance of respiratory indicators in the light of the following criteria: the clinical analysis of the content of speech uttered in psychiatric interviews, physiological (electromyographic) reactions, the effect of neuroleptic drugs, and the syndromes consisting of reactions to these and hesitation behaviour as thrown up in a factor analysis.

The hypothesis that the rate of expiration (ER) measuring output of speech per breath is an indicator of the strength of control, and that the breath rate during speech (SBR) is a measure of the intensity of excitation was borne out by the results. Increase in pause time (P) with the increase of cognitive complexity of verbal tasks was found to be inversely related to SBR and directly to ER. Evidence was obtained from a factor analysis of an inhibition-excitation factor of personality manifesting itself in speech-breathing behaviour as well as in this extra pause time during speech involving such complex cognitive activity. The two types of gap which break the flow of speech output, i.e. the hesitation and breath pauses, seem thus to be extensions into behaviour of the duality of functions which are involved when speech is being produced.

E

Conclusion

The study of the dynamics of speech production must, by its very nature, amount to a study of speech as mentation in the Hughlings Jackson sense. Spontaneity of utterance that goes beyond exclamation and interjection calls for acts of choice and decision at the semantic as well as linguistic levels. The observation and analysis of this process represents, therefore, a particular approach to the study of thinking, using speech as the observable link in the chain of generative events. If the investigations reported here are regarded in this light, they lend support to the following notions: (a) that for any given capacity time and tonus, the latter understood as a condition of readiness[9] and manifesting itself as effort, are the basic conditions for effective thinking; that these are functions and aspects of the neurophysiology and body chemistry of the thinking organism as it responds to stimulation from the environment. However specialized the cerebral cortex, the form and complexity, the style and intellectual quality of its product have been shown to be the fruit of processes in the organism as a whole. (b) That time is an entity actively made by the organism as well as granted to it, the latter being an external condition, the former a function of tonus, whether this tonus be primary, a manifestation of the neurophysiological response to body chemistry (the set or initial tension state), or secondary, induced in reaction to external or internal stimuli and as a result of feedback from external and internal sources.

(a) The Dynamic Relationship Between Time and Tonus

To be productive, time available must become time used. When time available for the conception and verbal planning of cartoon interpretations was extended, it was utilized for cortical activity and resulted in a linguistic product of heightened intellectual quality (see Chapter 4).

If efficiency (cognitive or otherwise) is a function of optimal cortical tonicity then time is a necessary though not sufficient condition for its deployment (see Chapter 7).

Equally the same tonic condition given insufficient time for functioning remains unproductive. If tonus and time are both indispensable are they also inter-dependent?

The category of "time used" as compared with "time available" arises from introducing the active organism into an objectively given

122

time quantity. A further and different category is time "made" or time "found". This is still objective time; it is measurable by world chronometers as distinct from physiological or psychological i.e. of subjective time. But time "found" or "made" implies that the organism has used initiative, has rearranged and reorganized its activities so as to make time available. Thus those subjects who, when asked to interpret the meaning of cartoons in a concise form, delayed their response more came up with the better solution to the task. Similarly, simultaneous translators though constrained within a fixed time span have on occasion restructured and redistributed the total time available to them for listening and translating; they have changed the proportions between speech and silence as given in the input, have crammed their output without loss of text into less time and extended the time of non-speech. They have actively "made" time against the odds of a fixed quantity of time and output to be transmitted.

Time "made" is normally made for use and therefore being used (except when something goes wrong). Time "available", time "used" and time "made" may be regarded as three stages of intensity in the utilization and exploitation of the commodity of time. Waste—normal use—and intensive cultivation and exploitation, these degrees of intensity in time utilization (as in soil cultivation) are degrees of effort, of the act of utilization invested in the act of speech production.

Here we meet with the category of "human work" projecting between man and the physico-chemical environment "use-objects" (Gebrauchsobjekte) of which language is one—others being clothing, gardens and "cultural objects" such as books or musical instruments (Merleau-Ponty, 1965).

The simultaneous translator "making" pause time within a given total time of utterance at the cost of the time, but not quantity, of speech is engaged in productive cultural work. This is perhaps one of the most difficult forms of making time; but even when time available is not a fixed quantity, nor speech material to be produced pre-determined as is the case in spontaneous speech, speakers still "make" time by expanding their pauses of hesitation, though working under less stringent conditions. They are free to trade in time for a reduction in quantity of speech produced as was done in the interpretation of cartoons (Chapter 3) or to lengthen the total time of the discourse. This situation seems to stimulate a tonic state, e.g. when S.I.* did not decrease under Chlorpromazine in the interpretations of cartoons as distinct from the interviews. The indication is that the increased tonus due to situations of challenge leads to defensive action, i.e. to a correction in response to feedback. Thus a "functional system",[10] in the Anokhin sense, seems to

* (Subordination index).

be set to steer towards high level intellectual performance. Speech action would be delayed in exchange for cognitive activity with the resulting increase in the intellectual value of the product. The behavioural manifestations of this system constitute Factor 1 as extracted from the factor analysis described in Chapter 9.

The temporal properties of duration, order and succession play an essential part in this system. Its dynamic nature was described by Ukhtomskii (cited from Luria, 1966) who concludes that, "Co-ordination in the time, speed and rhythm of action, and indeed, in the periods at which the various moments of the reaction occur creates a functionally unified 'center' from spatially different groups . . ."

"Each link of this system plays its own differential role (providing the 'motor task', the spatial and kinetic scheme of the movement, the feedback of signals from the effect of the completed action, etc.). It is only by the close interaction of the elements of this functional system that its essential plasticity and self-regulation can be assured."

The operation of the functional system geared to the task of generating spontaneous speech must manifest itself in tonal changes and their temporal arrangements, and the question how these are interrelated, is therefore relevant to our discourse. How closely time and tonus are linked is seen if we consider that of the two fundamental aspects of time —succession and duration—succession, to be orderly, requires the functioning of control. The grammatical requirements ruling the order of speech units were reduced in complexity and degree of structure under the influence of Chlorpromazine, but the reduction of tonus thus effected did not involve extra duration (Chapter 5). Orderly succession of verbal elements held in suspense was a function of tonus, but not of hesitancy. This relation between succession and effort (tonus) is in keeping with other evidence. Fraisse (1964, p. 97) reports that, "Cortical lesions can prevent the organisation of successive stimuli into temporal forms . . ." and ". . . that neuroses can reduce the efficiency of this organisation of elements when they are complex and require an effort to be perceived correctly". Delay (1942), too, speaks of memory disturbances through inability to make the intellectual effort which permits the ordering of memories (Fraisse, 1964, p. 167). "Our temporal horizon", says Fraisse, "is a perspective constructed from indications provided by the temporal signs of our efforts to organise our memories by calling on all the available principles of temporal organisations" (p. 167). The reduction of tension after lobotomy results in a lack of interest in the future ". . . which is not a loss of the ability to foresee but a reduction in the capacity to make the effort through which the different temporal perspectives can be envisaged together" (Porot, 1947; Jones, 1949 (from Fraisse, p. 191)).

Of the two aspects of time, succession and duration, succession and the organization and anticipation of successive events thus requires effort and therefore a corresponding tonal basis in the organism.

While syntactic operations require extra effort, but accomplish the temporal organization of verbal elements without requiring extra delay time, lexical and semantic operations require extra delay time. What is the position concerning extra effort or increase in tonus?

What seemed to emerge (Goldman-Eisler, 1965) was that the efficiency of the intellectual operation of generalizing was a matter of tonus being optimal rather than maximal.

But, here too time and tonus are related. When a surplus of tonicity as indicated by a high RBR is reduced, speech action under intellectual challenge can be postponed and the intellectual quality improves (Chapter 9). When a medium (or low) level of initial tension, reflected in a medium (or low) RBR, is reduced, the intellectual quality of the product deteriorates. The relation between tonus and duration seems to have the form of an inverse U function, that between tonus and succession to be linear. Subjects under the influence of Chlorpromazine, i.e. when relaxed, showed a reduction of sentence complexity ($S.I.$) irrespective of their level of RBR. Subjects under the influence of this drug increased or decreased their pausing time in complex cognitive speech concurrently with the intellectual quality of their product in accordance with their level of RBR.

It seems therefore that the highest level of intellectual and semantic function as distinct from the exercise of syntactic skill is selective and specific (Anokhin) in transmuting tonal properties. Thus a tonic condition which may have a non-specific effect on one kind of operation, such as the serial ordering of verbal elements in accordance with grammatical requirements, i.e. on syntactic operations, has a specific finely graded effect on complex semantic operations. To achieve optimum semantic performance tonus there must be relaxed control, neither rigid nor flabby. Semantic creation, i.e. thought, requires time and during spontaneous speech time needs to be *made*; this seems to call for an attitude, a set tolerating unfilled time and balancing the drive towards filling time with verbal activity; it requires care and a capacity for discontinuing utterance in the service of its meaningful though delayed continuation on the one hand against nonchalance as to how it is to be filled on the other.

(b) Time in Syntactic and Semantic Operations

The distinction between the two tonic states and the two aspects of time attached to the syntactic and semantic operations is important.

So far analysis in terms of temporal aspects has concentrated on syntactic operations, in the first place inspired by Karl Lashley. His illuminating analysis of the problem of syntax as one of serial ordering in time of elements organized hierarchically similar to skilled acts generally, suffers from the over-extension of his generalization. Thus the last sentence in his celebrated paragraph reads:

"The analysis of the nervous mechanisms underlying order in the more primitive acts may contribute ultimately to the solution even of the physiology of logic." The assumption behind this statement, that syntactic and logical operations belong to the same class generally, is perpetuated in present linguistic and psycholinguistic argument. Miller (1964), for instance, in reformulating the Lashley thesis in terms of "flexible postponement" describes the phenomenon as follows: "What I mean by flexible postponement, however, is at least two degrees more complicated than simple delay. The kind of task I have in mind would demand that one class of activities be held in abeyance until another class has been brought to a successful conclusion. The delay period, in other words, is filled with some intervening behaviour that must be completed before the postponed reaction can occur." And further, Miller relates language to the making of tools, and speaks of ". . . the selective pressure that favoured toolmakers also favouring those individuals who could formulate and execute hierarchically organised plans in which the tools played a role". Miller fails to keep up this distinction between formulating and executing plans, but continues: "My argument is that this ability is exactly what was needed to make language possible. It is just this flexible ability to organise behaviour sequentially that is a unique and indispensable feature of human language." Here again we meet with the substitution of sequential organization for the act of formulation. This is spelled out as follows: "The general proposition I want to leave with you can be summarised quite simply. The first is that the kind of planful organisation that underlies all complex human behaviour is quite similar to the *syntactic* [our italics] organisation that underlies language." The first and most basic ability, according to Miller, which must be present is an ability for flexible postponement. The precision of Miller's definition of this delay as one that ". . . is filled with some intervening behaviour that must be completed before the postponed reaction can occur", enables us to see clearly that we are dealing here with a distinctly different type of delay than the one involved in pauses of hesitation. In these the delay is a total one, the time is unfilled, emptied of peripheral verbal behaviour; it is a time of external inactivity and requires an ability to postpone verbal activity altogether, and a capacity to maintain silence. Formulating as distinct from executing verbal plans, i.e.

preparing for and anticipating activity in the future (however near) as distinct from carrying out the activity, was found to require time for inaction; the silence of planning must therefore precede flexible postponement, i.e. the delays of some verbal acts in favour of others as part of the organization of elements in serial order. As a result of the experiments described in this volume, the serial ordering of elements was shown to be a matter of alertness related to the organized execution of peripheral acts; the semantic generation of language on the other hand, e.g. in word choice or the interpretation and creation of meaning to be a matter of suspending peripheral acts and concentrating on central activity.

Katz and Fodor (1964), in mapping the domain of a semantic theory, argued that a speaker's ability to interpret sentences ". . . provides the empirical data for a construction of such a theory, just as construction of a grammar draws upon empirical data supplied by the exercise of a speaker's ability to distinguish well-formed sentences from ungrammatical strings, to recognise syntactic ambiguity, and to appreciate relations between sentence types". It was precisely this interpretative ability of speakers which was enlisted in the cartoon experiment. The different correlates of pause behaviour which distinguish the operation of interpreting meaning from that of embedding clauses in sentences appear to range from the level of linguistic analysis to that of the behaviour and neurophysiological set of speakers. This and the importance of the duration of pauses in the semantic and of the succession of vocal elements in the syntactic acts point to an intrinsic division between semantic and syntactic operations.

(c) The Functional Integration of the Syntactic/Semantic Dichotomy

At the same time we must contemplate that while there is such a division when the utterance is regarded statically, dynamically semantic and syntactic operations may be phases in a continuous generative process. Two stages have been distinguished (Kainz, 1954 and others) in the generation of speech advancing towards the completed utterance: (a) that of the inner speech, of the conception of the content to be verbalized as well as its formulation and (b) of external speech, the linguistic and phonetic execution of the inner speech. These two stages are related as is strategy to tactics or planning to execution. It seems from all the characteristics of the steep and shallow slopes in our analysis of the hesitancy/fluency cycle that they correspond to these two stages of spontaneous cognitive speech. How do syntactic operations relate to these two gradients?

It seems that the planning (strategy)/executing (tactics) axis runs orthogonally to the semantic/syntactic one. If the planning/executing axis can be identified with Factor 1 emerging from the factor analysis reported, and can be related to semantic operations (Factor 1 being saturated with hesitancy (P) and related to intellectual function), the syntactic operations (independent of hesitancy) seem to have little in common with either Factor 1 or Factor 2. The latter, a personality factor of individuals' arousal state, appeared to determine the direction of the effect of Chlorpromazine on intellectual function (Chapter 9), whilst the effect of this drug on syntactic operations was non-selective (Chapter 5). This would indicate that the tonicity involved in syntactic operations is a more fleeting phenomenon than the two personality factors of Control, Inhibition, Effort (F. 1) and of individual's arousal state (F. 2), a tonicity subject not only to drugs but to verbal and intellectual tasks and adjustable according to their challenges (Chapter 5).

It would appear that already at the stage of strategy and of inner speech all operations, semantic including lexical, *and* syntactic, take place in a kind of functional symbiosis, dovetailing, interacting and reacting to feedback. Lashley (also Kainz) speaks of words and word groups as offering themselves, springing to attention to be arranged in syntactic order to fit into well-learned schemata and model structures of sentences. Miller's flexible postponement would presuppose the presence of syntactic schemata, like scaffoldings, awaiting the interpolation of the lexical units postponed to await their turn. Semantic operations would stem from the prelinguistic anticipatory stages of intention and conception and evolve into composition by projecting lexical elements into syntactic schemata thus creating semantically novel sentences.

The conception of ready-made sentence schemata, models of sentences or modules implies that they are selected in one piece so to speak, that they are not constructed from individual lexical elements—and this would account for the fluency of speakers irrespective of their complexity, in the same way as efficiency in mass production is a matter of use of prefabricated units. It explains the fact that in simultaneous translation no delay was associated with the translation of highly complex sentences in the source as long as their structure was left unchanged in the target language, while a new sentence structure, even when simpler than the original one, resulted in hesitation. What seemed to take time was choosing a *different* schema from the one presented, a complex process involving the rejection of the structure as received, the decision to deviate from it and the choice of an alternative syntactic form. Further study is needed of the durations specific to these acts.

(d) Respiratory Behaviour and the Levels of Organization of Spoken Language

One mechanism through which cognitive activity and the biological functioning of the organism as a whole has been specifically shown to interact is respiration. Here two levels of interference with the resting breath rate could be observed to operate as a result of the act of speaking (this resting breath rate measured in the waking state itself was shown to be the result of the interference with the sleeping breath rate by the steady state of waking alertness). The act of speaking as such disturbs the biological rhythm of pulmonary ventilation and O_2 absorption, by subjecting it to the grouping of speech units according to the structural requirements of language. The linguistic level of interaction thus interferes with the placing of breath intakes, substituting for the biological regularity of the resting breath rate (RBR) the structural determination of the speech breath rate (SBR). The rate of breathing, however, as distinct from its rhythm, does not seem to be affected by the fact of speech production in itself as the measurements comparing the reading and resting breath rates have shown (p. 116).

The rate of breathing is modified as a result of the interference not by the level of linguistic organization, but by changes in the complexity of cognitive activity, and in accordance with the speaker's functioning along the inhibition/excitation continuum. In accordance with these changes a second displacement of breath intake was observed, and this time the synchrony of the placing of breath intakes with the structural requirements of language was disturbed as part of the general arrest of peripheral activity which accompanies complex cognitive operations.

Respiratory behaviour studied in terms of the placement and frequency of breathing thus shows that the organism, while operating at different levels in the hierarchy of total organization according to the different degrees of cognitive complexity involved in the production of speech, acts as a whole. The principle of functional unity seems accordingly to extend to high level psycholinguistic activity. The organism as a whole seems set tonically and arrested temporally in accordance with the difficulty of whatever cognitive task presents itself to speakers.

Appendix I

Illustrations of such continuous recordings are shown in the diagrams below. These were derived from an experiment in which three psychiatrists of Maudsley Hospital (who will be referred to as D_1, D_2, and D_3) took part. They were chosen on the basis of a judged difference in their conversational activity, the experimenter predicting essentially different scores for D_1 on the one hand and D_2 and D_3 on the other. A group of patients, five reserved (four cases of depression and one of uncertain diagnosis), and five talkative (four cases of anxiety and one uncertain), were then selected to be interviewed by all the three doctors in rotation. There were thus 30 interviews altogether. Any errors arising from the order of interviewing, that is, from the fact that patients would respond differently according to whether they were interviewed for the first, second or third time, irrespective of which doctor interviewed them, were controlled by putting them in random order.

The three interviewers were thus compared against a constant stimulus background. Furthermore, in order to make the interviews comparable, a common aim was set, namely to describe and diagnose the patients' present mental state. The doctors were, within those limits, given freedom to use their own personal technique and approach.

These interviews were recorded both on the interaction chronograph (Chapple, 1942), giving a continuous record of the length of time taken up in action (speech and relevant gesture) and in silence by each of the speakers, and also on the speech recorder.

The following results, reported elsewhere in detail (Goldman-Eisler, 1952), emerged from the analysis of the time recording (interaction chronograph).

Interviewers showed themselves to behave consistently, irrespective of the type of patient interviewed, with respect to two of the three measures taken: (a) bs/ds, i.e., the ratio of the total number of short silences (bs)* to the total number of long silences (ds)† in the speech of the interviewer, and (b) $A + S$, i.e., the average period comprising an action (A) plus its subsequent silence period (S). As regards the third measure used, namely AT, i.e., the total amount of time that was spent in action (talk and gesture) expressed as a percentage of the total time of the interview, the interviewers showed themselves consistent in rela-

* Less than 5 sec.   † Five seconds and over.

130

tion to each other, but all adjusted themselves to about the same extent when passing from the reticent group of patients to the talkative.

The patients' conversational behaviour was consistent with respect to bs/ds, and AT. While the latter value, i.e. the amount of time spent in talking, proved independent of the interviewers, the bs/ds score (activity rate) showed itself sensitive according to which of the three doctors was the interviewer. $A + S$ (conversational tempo) did not show reliability but seemed subject to interviewers' influence.

In short, the interviewers showed themselves more rigid with respect to activity rate (bs/ds) and tempo or rhythm of interaction while being highly flexible with respect to the amount of time they talked in an interview. Patients were most rigid with respect to the amount of time and activity and seemed subject to influence in respect of tempo or rhythm of interaction.

The diagrams based on the continuous recordings show that the consistency reported above of certain relations between overall measures of time of silence and speech does not rest there. Individual differences are specific in what one may call dynamic expression (see Fig. 1).

The curves shown are of cumulative plottings of the differences between time of activity (speech and gesture) and inactivity (silence without gesture), along the baseline of succeeding exchanges. If the former is A (action) and the latter is S (silence) for each succeeding exchange the point is determined by the sum of differences. Thus point 1 is $A_1 - S_1$, point 2: $(A_1 - S_1) + (A_2 - S_2)$, point 3: $[(A_1 - S_1) + (A_2 - S_2)] + (A_3 - S_3)$ etc. Where A is larger than S, the shape of the curve is ascending; where S is larger, it is descending, and where A and S are similar, it remains near the baseline. Changes in this relationship determine variations in the trend of the curve (the dotted vertical lines indicate the passage of 5 min).

The overall fact of ascendance or descendance of the doctors is a function of the interlocutor. Thus the doctor's curves are less descending when talking to the taciturn depressive patient, and more so when faced with the talkative manic or anxious patient. As their aim is always to make patients talk, they must always be descending. Patients, on the other hand, behave in accordance with their disposition. But in the particular shape of ascendance or descendance, the points at which momentum is gained or lost shows properties characteristic of the individual, doctor or patient.

Thus some of the ascenders start with high gain in A over S, but lose momentum later on, as e.g. P_6, P_8, P_9 and P_{10}, whilst P_7 gains momentum later, with a balanced start. Even where the strongly active interference by D_3 cuts down the overall output of P_7, the characteristic shape over time remains unchanged.

Of descending patients compare P_4 with his characteristic initial balanced activity and loss of momentum only after the first 5 min, and the unrelieved passivity and constant decrement between A and S in P_3.

The same tendency towards dynamic individuality of conversational activity is also observable in the curves representing the doctors' behaviour, in particular D_1 and D_2. Thus there is a consistent tendency all through their interviews for D_1 to gain in descendancy as the interview goes on, whilst D_2 becomes more active in its course. D_3 seemed more variable, though there is a tendency to maintain the initial trend, particularly with talkative patients.

The management of temporal relationships as a highly personal factor is thus shown to be revealed only in the successiveness of recorded phenomena and their evolution in time.

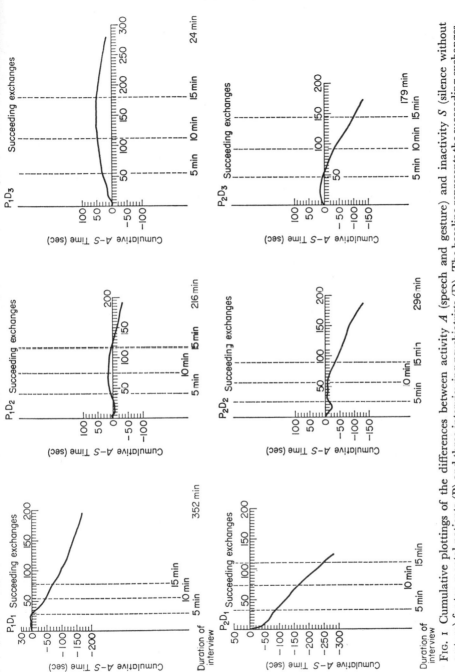

FIG. 1 Cumulative plottings of the differences between activity A (speech and gesture) and inactivity S (silence without gesture) for ten mental patients (P) and three interviewing psychiatrists (D). The baseline represents the succeeding exchanges. PD = patient talking to doctor; DP = doctor talking to patient.

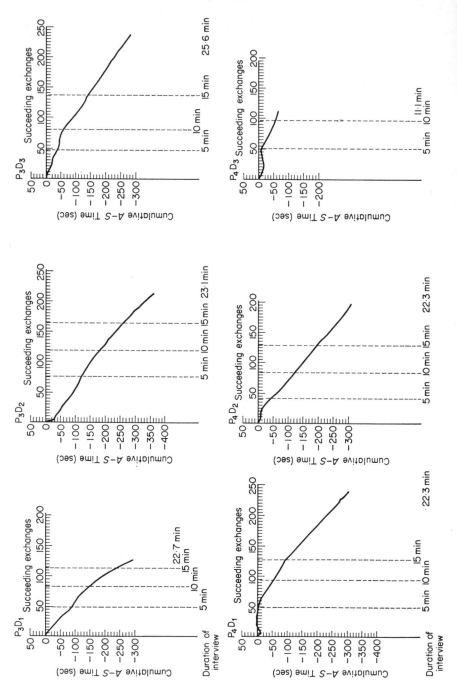

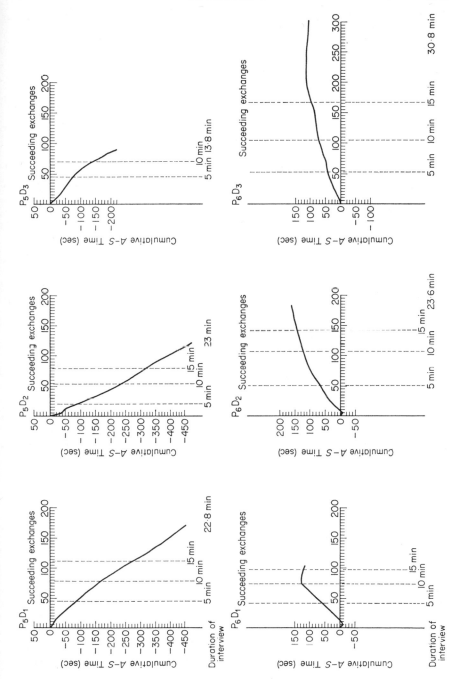

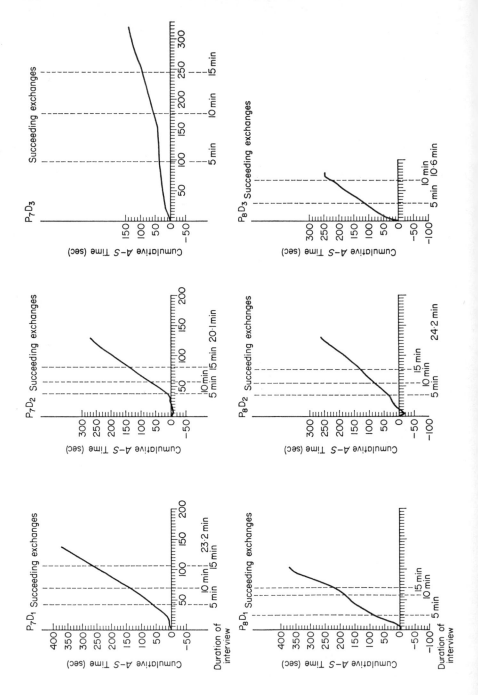

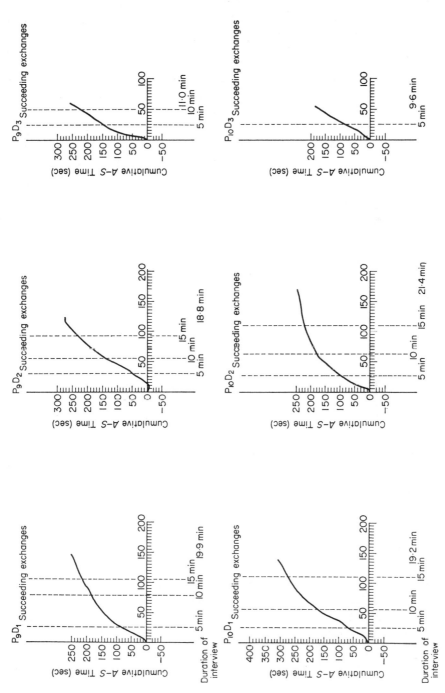

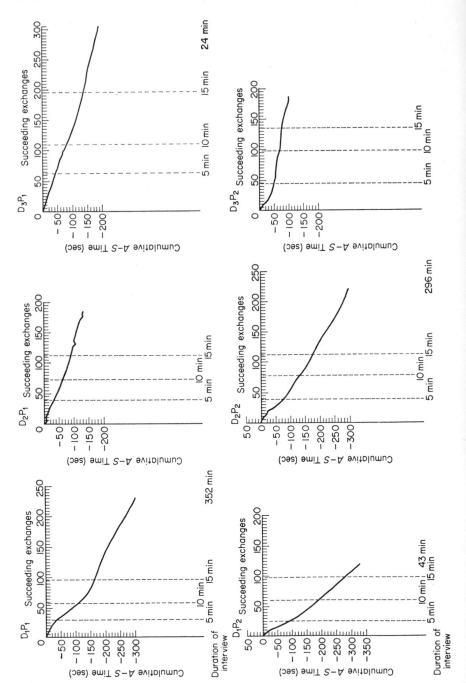

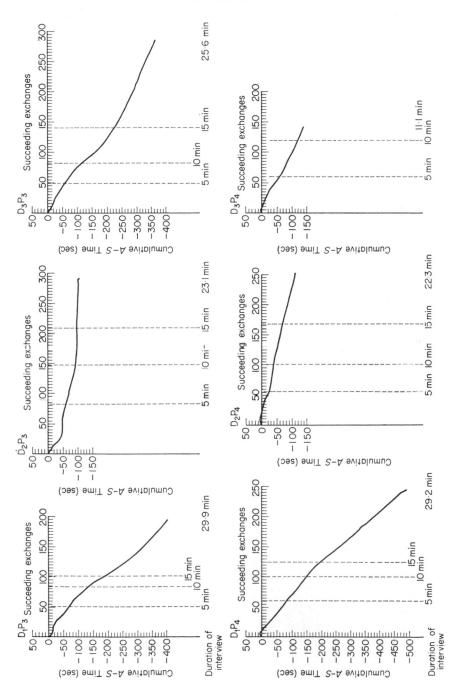

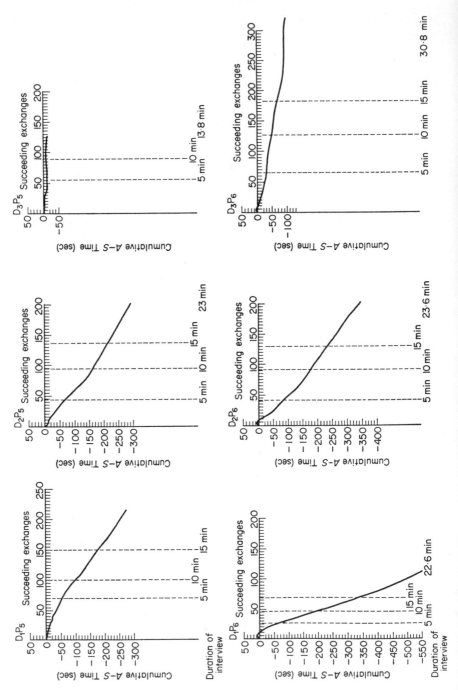

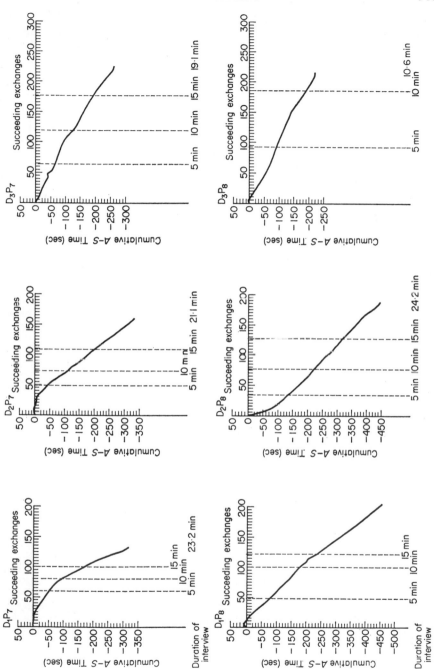

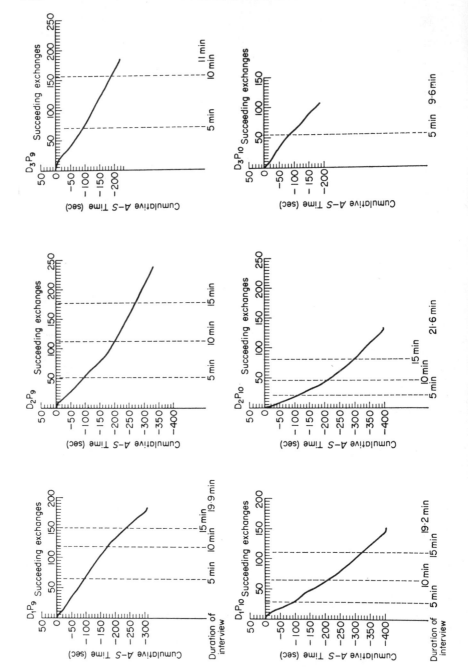

Appendix II

Recorded Signal Detector

This instrument was designed by J. West in the Laboratory of the Department of Phonetics, University College London for use in conjunction with an Ampex 351 tape recorder and an Ediswan model EPR pen oscillograph; it is intended for one or two channel operation.

Each channel comprises a 600-ohm stepped potentiometer giving a total of 10 steps of attenuation, each of 2 dB. The attenuator output is fed to a non-blocking amplifier which drives a bridge rectifier and smoothing circuit having a 20 millisecond time-constant. The smoothed rectifier output is fed into a transistor, the base-emitter diode of which acts as a voltage limiter, giving approximately equal switch-off delays for small and large audio input signals. The transistor collector circuit contains a relay which in the energized condition connects the pen coil to 8·0 V r.m.s., 50 c/s and in the rest position connects it to a 1 KΩ damping resistance. The minimum detected signal is 28 dB below 2·0 r.m.s., the latter being the normal peak output from the Ampex 351 line output.

The two channels are identical. The 18 V D.C. supply is obtained from an Advance DCT 1 power supply which has a large reserve of power available.

OPERATION

It is assumed that any input above a certain intensity will be regarded as "signal", and everything below as "noise". The determination of the level at which the discrimination must be made is arbitrary and must be made in the light of experience. Once a level has been established, however, it is important that it can be consistently maintained and to this end the following recommendations are made:

(i) Apart from the obvious necessity to exclude extraneous noise during recording, particular care should be taken to avoid hum pick-up, as the detector circuit is much more sensitive than the ear at hum frequencies.

(ii) A few seconds of recorded tone on each channel at the beginning of each session will provide a reference against which the replay

143

volume setting can be checked, each time an analysis is made. By giving care to the reproduced level, quite accurate repetition should be possible.

(iii) The tone should be recorded at 0 v.u. on the meter, and on re-play, the gain should be adjusted to again give this reading.

(iv) Attenuator settings should be noted on the pen recordings.

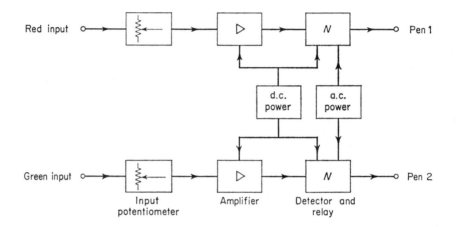

Record of text and simultaneous translation.

Appendix III

Goldman-Eisler and Mendoza, 1965

The need for the following equipment was felt in 1957–8 after the experiments concerned with the function of pausing in speech proved successful in that they showed that this function was concerned with the generation of information in speech, and that pausing could be interpreted as behavioural manifestation of cognitive processes taking place in the course of speech production (Goldman-Eisler, 1958c, 1961d).

As the analysis of speech in terms of speaking and pauses was Goldman-Eisler's scientific contribution, and therefore new both in concept and method, no equipment was known to deal with this kind of speech analysis. The original investigations were based on data gained through transforming the sound impulses derived from the tape recorder which were transformed into graphic representation of periods of sound and silence using a rectifier device (Goldman-Eisler, 1958c). This involved a very time-consuming and cumbersome evaluation of the records by measuring the tape length between the records of the impulses in order to obtain the numerical values required for the calculation analysis of the data.

The equipment was required to save the labour involved in this operation and automatize it; in other words, the task was to design equipment which would record, count, totalize and print periods of pausing as well as speaking directly in precise, chosen fractions of seconds. The equipment was designed by R. Mendoza.

The particular problem to be solved was to make use of the Hewlett-Packard Decade Counter AC-4A/B and the Hewlett-Packard Digital Recorder 560A, both these instruments having been made freely available to the Department of Phonetics by courtesy of the U.S. Air Force which entailed a considerable saving in cost. The circuit described can, of course, be adapted for use with other counters. The following description and figure show how the problem was solved.

The speech under examination is fed from a tape recorder to reference level meter calibrated in decibels. This enables the speech level to the analyser to be adjusted allowing for recorded level variations. An additional attenuator is provided for controlling the input to the audio amplifier feeding the detector. The time integrated pulse from the detector is fed to a D.C. amplifier and then shaped by a Schmitt trigger circuit. These pulses are now ready for transfer to the Electronic Counter for totalizing.

Speech time is measured by feeding a signal suitably amplified from a 100 c/s generator which in turn is derived from the mains supply. The 100 c/s signal is fed to a speech time gate which is itself switched by the time integrated speech pulse from the Schmitt trigger. By suitably setting the controls on the electronic counter, a direct reading in time units is thus attainable.

In a similar manner a time-integrated pause pulse is fed to a pause time gate which switches through to the electronic counter the 100 c/s reference, thus clocking up pause times on the counter.

A digital recorder prints on a paper tape the displays obtained from the electronic counter. A remote control box enables a print command voltage to be fed to the recorder when required, for example when totalizing pulses, speech and pause times, over a certain derived portion of the speech recording.

To facilitate ease of operation an additional remote switch is provided to disconnect the input to the counter while at the same time stopping the tape recorder. This enables the operator to stop the recording where required without recording the unwanted pause time which stopping the recording would normally produce.

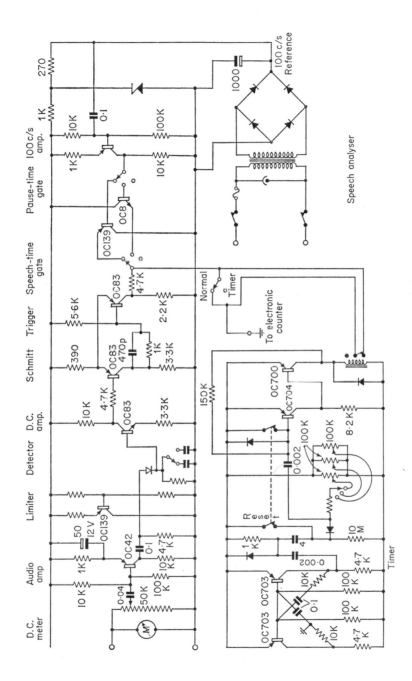

Notes

Note 1 (p. 28)

Ichlondsky (1930), writing on the relations between neuropsychic activity and language, describes this event as follows:

"Concerning the dependence of neuropsychic activity in general and thinking in particular on the symbols of language: words form the complex of forms within which come to pass our thoughts, feelings and wishes and which keep our neuropsychic responses in a firm grip. Thus language can play a positive as well as a negative role in the process of thinking and neuropsychic creation.

"The interrelations between neuropsychic activity and language evolved in such a way that both factors were cause as well as effect, of course not at the same time, but in succession whereby one factor stabilized the other and thus furthered continued development.

"The formation of verbal symbols was of greatest importance for the adequacy of neuropsychic responses, because it stabilized these responses: as the neuropsychic response became tied to a certain verbal form, it became permanently fixed and lasting; it was prevented from vanishing and could, through repetition, be reinforced to such an extent that it became the starting point of new connections and new responses. The effect of the word moreover was that a response once stimulated left behind a deeper material trace in the central nervous system—a path to which new connections, new conditioned reflexes could be joined.

"Without this fixation of elaborated neuropsychic responses, viz. of the trace underlying them, their enduring existence would be impossible.

"But this was not the only significance of the word. It could also be the prime mover and initiate neuropsychic responses.

"Clearly there is quantitatively a great difference between the conditions of language evolution in cases where stimuli from a variety of analysers participate in the process of language formation, and cases in which stimuli from only one analyser prevail: the more analysers contribute to the process of verbalization, the stronger and more reliable will become the conditioned reflexes which underlie the neuropsychic responses.

"Language is a great complex of special conditioned stimuli most closely connected with the corresponding neuropsychic responses. A

149

complete correspondence between language on the one hand and thinking on the other can exist only as long as the thinking fits into that
mean of neuropsychic achievement which is covered by the linguistic
expression.

"This is predominantly the case in everyday thinking which is the
product of a collective effort, viz. of the phylogenetic evolution. *It is
quite different in the case of strongly marked individual thinking, as e.g. in profound deliberations of scientific nature, or philosophical contemplations and similar.
Here a strong discrepancy must make itself felt between the individual thought
advancing on new grounds and the conservation of language which is a common
denominator in representing neuropsychic achievement* [Author's italics].

"The words in their role as conditioned stimuli lack the capacity of
fixing newly evolving pathways and connections in the brain matter
(cortex). Moreover the existing word being the conditioned stimulus of
an old connection does not permit it to be corrected without effort by
the neuropsychic advance and the new pathways it necessitates. As the
existing word learned through centuries and acting as conditioned
stimulus continues the old pathway, this cannot successfully be inhibited, as the new stimulation and as new connections would require.

"But as the pathway to be extinguished has in the past been tied to a
certain word or expression, this verbal symbol must always revive the
old path and impede the imprinting of the new path counteracting it,
and continue to weaken it, diverting from it energy by way of negative
induction. In this way it unnoticeably effects a more or less extensive
return from the newly conceived to the old and renders difficult the
evolution of new concepts.

"Language being a complex of imprinted conditioned stimuli pro-
motes but also inhibits creative (scientific) thinking" [Author's own
translation].

Note 2 (p. 29)

This is in line with present-day research. The evolution of left hemisphere dominance in speech conforms with Hughlings Jackson's division
between the automatic and voluntary service of words if these are also
understood to be stages in the ontogony of the use of words as was
shown by Luria (1961).

Thus Lenneberg (1966) in surveying the field cites extensive evidence
showing that cerebral lateralization of the speech function is a relatively
plastic phenomenon and that no lateralization seems to be present
before age two or three. He reaches the conclusion that "there is a
period that lasts to about ten or twelve during which cerebral lateralization for speech is gradually established but may still be pushed back

into the right hemisphere if the left hemisphere is disturbed. After puberty, lateralization is normally firmly established to the left, and the right hemisphere is no further involved in speech functions; lesions to the left interfere with speech, but lesions to the right do not".

Note 3 (p. 74)

Anokhin (1960) writes: ". . . observations show that the desynchronizing effect of the reaction to the novelty, i.e. the appearance of a pronounced orienting, investigatory reaction, is directly dependent on the initial state of the experimental animal. The creation of a biologically negative dominant by means of preliminary applications of pain stimuli under the given experimental conditions aids in especially intensifying the activating effect of the reticular formation on the cerebral cortex under the action of a new stimulus and yields a highly pronounced desynchronization of cortical electrical activity.

"Contrariwise, a dominance of alimentary activity, i.e. a biologically positive state, also created beforehand, does not, yield such desynchronization under the action of the indifferent, i.e. a new, stimulus.

"Thus, these observations persuade us that the biological quality of the initial state of the animal's nervous system determines the force of the desynchronizing action of the indifferent stimulus.

"And this means that the new stimulus mobilizes the activating mechanisms of the reticular formation in accordance with the form of biological activity that either dominates or facilitates the formation of the reaction at the given moment.

". . . There is every reason to believe that the qualitatively different biological reactions (orienting reaction, defensive reaction and alimentary reaction) excite in the reticular formation different complexes of neural elements which are specific for them. These neural elements, in their turn, exert a specific activating influence on the cerebral cortex mobilizing in it intracortical connections adequate to the given reaction. The selective effect of aminasine (chlorpromazine) as an adrenolytic poison, shows that this difference in the various biological complexes of the reticular formation is likely to proceed so far that it may become constitutional, i.e. with different chemical features and different metabolism of the corresponding neural elements. It is the selective effect of these different complexes on the cortical electrical activity and the selective involvement of the cellular elements of the cortex in desynchronization that we call the specific activating effect of the reticular formation on the cerebral cortex.

". . . It is well known that, as an adrenalitic agent, chlorpromazine blocks the rostral part of the reticular formation and thus prevents the pain impulses from reaching the cerebral cortex (Agafonov, Dell, Roth-baller). It would seem that on the basis of these facts we should assume that aminasine (chlorpromazine) must also inhibit the epileptic discharges of the cells located in the reticular formation. However, experience indicates the reverse.

". . . How are we to conceive the mechanism of such action of chlorpromazine? It seems to me that at the present stage of development of our ideas concerning the functions of reticular formations we are warranted in giving an explanation to this mechanism.

"The sympathoadrenal system and central integrator, the dorsal hypothalamus and the adrenergic substratum of the brain stem, function particularly actively when in states of 'tension' . . . the adrenergic system naturally maintains these other functions in a somewhat inhibited state.

". . . If the spinal cord is cut beneath the medulla oblongata at this moment when all the reflexes are inhibited, the spinal reflexes are restored. The mechanism of the phenomenon could also be explained from the point of view of the dynamic interaction of the heterogeneous functional systems of the reticular formation. It is well known that there are two types of reticular influences on spinal co-ordination: facilitating and inhibiting. We are quite warranted in assuming that being very active, the adrenergic system depresses the inhibitory function of the reticular system of the medulla oblongata. It follows that blocking the adrenergic system with chlorpromazine must release this inhibitory function. In this conception the extremely paradoxical fact of chlorpromazine action in a downward direction, as was shown in our laboratory, is fully accounted for.

"By comparing all these facts we have come to the conclusion that the biological specificity of the stimulus (pain, alimentary) now manifests itself in the specific electrical activity at the level of the reticular formation and this, in its turn, probably determines the peculiarity of the activating effect produced by the reticular formation on the cerebral cortex. This is demonstrated by the selective action of pharmacological agents on them."

Note 4 (p. 74)

The characteristic effect of this drug on normal human beings is one of producing a feeling of wakefulness and alertness; a change in mood to euphoria and elation; greater ability to concentrate; more initiative and self-confidence; and an overall feeling of well-being. These actions are due partly to its undoubted action as a cortical stimulant and probably partly to its action on the reticulo-activating system (Blair, 1958.)

Note 5 (p. 102)

Stetson's claim was criticized on the grounds of incompleteness in the correlation between chest pulse and syllable. Thus Kenneth L. Pike (1958) lists three exceptions to Stetson's statement that, "The syllable is one in the sense that it consists essentially of a single chest pulse, usually made audible by a vowel, which may be started or stopped by a chest movement.

"(1) Stetson failed to allow for a perceptual factor and was therefore forced to describe some groups of three sounds (two non-syllabic components and a vowel) as containing two syllables, when the ear does not hear them so; his recordings of the chest pulses included some that were too weak to register audibly. He says, for example, of PFEIL, and like words, that the second component sometimes becomes a 'preliminary silent syllable followed by a voiced syllable'. (2) He was confused by the spelling when he tried to describe consonant clusters. He says of certain of them, 'languages differ in their handling of these groups. The German spells a group TSCH, which the French spells TCH and the English CH!'. (3) He shows that another criterion than that of chest pulses may have led him to his conclusion when he grants the possibility of sound groups such as (aia) or (ala) being made with single chest pulses but constituting two syllables; in this case the oral movement would divide the syllables. He has no experimental evidence of the existence of this kind of syllable. Even if series of sounds of this type can be made with single chest pulses (and probably they can be, on the perceptual level at least), it appears preferable at least not to introduce a new criterion but to use one only—one based uniformly on strictural function. Introduction of a second type of articulatory criterion would probably undermine the consistency with which the first could be applied.

"Stricture within a continuum tends to prevent the egress of the air stream initiated by the pulmonic movement, and air pressure is built up behind these complete or partial strictures. The pressure accumulated in this way tends to slow down the movement of the initiator or to stop it entirely. When the strictures are released, the pressure is lessened, and the speed of the initiator movement increases. These alternations of initiator movements constitute the syllable pulse. . . . The majority of syllables are caused by changes of strictural interference with the air stream and initiator movement."

Ladefoged et al. (1958) write in a similar vein: "A single increase in tension spans a group of articulations including two vowels separated by a consonant closure (our records show that words such as 'pity' and 'around' may be spoken in this way); and sometimes there are two separate bursts of activity in what is normally regarded as a single syllable (e.g. in 'sport', 'stay', and other words beginning with a fricative followed by a plosive)".

"These results indicate that a consideration of the muscular activity which occurs when reading lists of words in a normal conversational style, is unlikely to lead us to the segments which are usually called syllables. Very often there is not even a correlation between the number of bursts of muscular activity and the number of segments perceived as syllables in an utterance.

"The bursts of activity of the internal intercostals were first noted by Stetson. They are very obvious in a simple utterance . . . but in normal speech they are far less evident. We made many recordings of the muscular activity which occurred when lists of words were read. These records show that each segment of speech which is perceived as a syllable is not necessarily accompanied by a separate burst of muscular activity. Stetson oversimplifies the situation by considering the activity of the intercostal muscles in terms of a series of 'ballistic movements', each of which either happens or does not happen. But in fact there are many other possibilities. Not only can the tension of the intercostal muscles be varied over a large range, but also there can be variations in the rate of change of tension."

The insufficiency of Stetson's general contention to cover each linguistic case stressed by these authors is, however, not relevant to the purpose of the measures as used here. Discrepancies between syllable and breath pulse, important to the phonetician who works with single sentences, did not seem a frequent enough event to invalidate the correlations based on large samples of speech as used in our case nor to contradict the statistical inferences drawn concerning the relation between the output of speech and the controlled retardation in the release of expiratory muscles of syllables per breath.

As indicators of the extension in the maintenance of the inspiratory position and resistance to the expiratory collapse of the breathing organ and therefore of a state of control and tension both the count of syllables as well as words have been found, as will be shown further on, to have validity when related to independent parameters.

The measure was found to be meaningful whether based on a count of words or syllables, which seems to be further support of its value as an average rather than as a measure of individual events.

Note 6 (p. 102)

Note the following facts from the physiology of speech production:
(a) The energy necessary for the production of articulate sound is

supplied by the expiratory phase of the breathing cycle.

(b) The current of expired air can be modified at will, owing to the cerebral connection with the respiratory centre.

(c) Ordinarily expiration is a mere cessation of the active process of inspiration. While the latter cannot be much prolonged—it being normally checked by the Hering-Breuer reflex—expiration takes place spontaneously and requires only to be regulated to form a continuous current of air of sufficient duration for the production of sound.

It is possible to increase this outgoing current of air either by expelling a stronger current of air following a moderate intake of breath by means of special expiratory activity involving muscular pressure, and so emptying the lungs, or by taking a deeper breath and so filling the lungs with a greater volume of air. An increased activity of the respiratory musculature of a voluntary and controlled kind is therefore necessary for both emphatic speech and acceleration.

Note 7 (p. 114)

P stands for the hesitation differential between speech under relaxed conditions (such as the description of cartoons) and intellectually demanding conditions (such as the interpretation of their meaning).

Note 8 (p. 119)

"The effect of sleep as a leveller of individual variation of *RBR* has been demonstrated by experiments with normals and psychiatric patients. In both these groups a narrowing of the band in sleep was quite apparent—this was due to the fact that there was a regression towards the mean: subjects with high *RBR* reduced their rate of breathing during sleep, while those with low *RBR* increased their rate. These findings suggest further that there is an automatic basic respiratory rate which, in the waking state, is modified by influences coming from higher centres. These effects in turn are presumed to be connected with the psychological state of the individual and to his personality attributes" (Skarbek, Ph.D. Thesis, unpublished).

Note 9 (p. 122)

Tonus, as used here, is to be understood in the sense of Bernstein's (1967) definition of the concept:

"The physiological data available on tonus has considerably extended the initial ideas on this topic which incorporated first only the idea of a condition of elasticity of the muscle fibres. Without any more accurate determinations tonus, in the vocabulary of the physiologists, began gradually to cover a very wide range of facts beginning with decerebrate rigidity and extending to Magnus and de Klein's tonus which has already been understood as a very generalized state of the motor periphery of preparation (in particular of the musculature of the neck and body) for the accomplishment of positions or movements.

"The older, static concept of tonus as physiological elasticity constricted and retarded the understanding of these phenomena. It seems that there is at present evidence enough to decide upon a judgment, perhaps preliminary, and to say the following about tonus.

"(a) Tonus as an ongoing physiological adaptation and organization of the periphery is not a condition of elasticity but a condition of readiness.

(b) Tonus is not merely a condition of the muscles but of the entire neuromuscular apparatus, including at least the final spinal synapse and the final common pathway.

(c) Tonus, from this point of view, is related to co-ordination as a state is to an action or as a precondition is to an effect."

Note 10 (p. 123)

Luria (1966) writes:

"The most significant feature of a functional system in this sense is that, as a rule, it is based on a complex dynamic 'constellation' of connections, situated at different levels of the nervous system, that, in the performance of the adaptive task, may be changed with the task itself remaining unchanged. Examples of functional systems are the apparently simple function of respiration which is actually a complex functional system, effected by a differential dynamic arrangement of nerve cells belonging to different levels of the nervous system. Equally the motor act . . . is a complex functional system. This system actually consists of many links with differentiated roles, and is capable of the highest degree of auto-regulation. Bernstein showed that movement is primarily determined by the 'motor task', which in loco-motion, goal-directed activity, or a symbolic act (e.g. a descriptive movement and writing) is formed at different levels and with the participation of different afferent systems. It is carried out not only by the cortical apparatuses, but also by the subcortical nuclei which provide the tonal background and co-ordination without which the movement would be impossible. . . . The structural basis of voluntary movement is a whole system of afferent and efferent links, situated in different parts and at different levels of the central nervous system."

References

Allport, Floyd H. (1955). "Theories of Perception and the Concept of Structure", John Wiley and Sons, Inc., New York. Chapman and Hall, Ltd, London.

Altschule, M. D. (1953). "Bodily Physiology in Mental and Emotional Disorders." Chapter: Respiration. Grune and Stratton, New York.

Anokhin, P. K. (1960). "On the Specific Action of the Reticular Formation on the Cerebral Cortex", *Int. J. clin. Neurophysiol.* Suppl. No. **13**, 257–270.

Anokhin, P. K. (1961). "A New Conception of the Physiological Architecture of Conditioned Reflex", *In* "Brain Mechanisms and Learning" (A. Fessard, R. W. Gerard, J. Konorski, J. F. Delafresnay, eds.), p. 189. Blackwell, Oxford.

Ax, A. F. (1953). "The Physiological Differentiation between Fear and Anger in Humans", *Psychosom. Med.* XV, No. **5**, 433–442.

Bell, E. H., Davidson, J. N., and Scarborough, H. (1965). "Textbook of Physiology and Biochemistry", E. and S. Livingstone Ltd, Edinburgh and London.

Bergson, H. (1912). "Creative Evolution", Macmillan and Co. Ltd, London.

Bernstein, N. (1967). "The Co-ordination and Regulation of Movements", Pergamon Press, Oxford, London and New York.

Blair, D. (1958). "Modern Drugs for the Treatment of Mentall Illness", Staples Press, London.

Bremer, F. (1966). "Neurophysiological Correlates of Mental Unity", *In* "Brain and Conscious Experience" (John C. Eccles, ed.), Springer-Verlag, Berlin, Heidelberg, New York.

Broadbent, D. E. (1958). "Perception and Communication", Pergamon Press, London, New York and Paris.

Bühler, K. (1933). "Sprachtheorie", Fischer, Jena.

Chapple, E. D. (1940). "Measuring Human Relations: An Introduction to the Study of the Interaction of Individuals", *Genet. Pyschol. Monogr.* 22.

Chapple, E. D. (1942). "The Measurement of Interpersonal Behavior", *Trans. N.Y. Acad. Sci.* **4**, 222–223.

Chomsky, N. (1957). "Syntactic Structures", Mouton and Co., The Hague.

Christiansen, B. (1965). "Studies in Respiration and Personality", Institute for Social Research, Oslo.

Ciofu, I. and Floru, R. (1965). Electroencephalographic Investigations of Set. Rev. Roumaine d. Sci. Soc., *Série de Psychologie*, **9**, 195.

Clausen, J. (1951). *Acta psychiat. et neurol. Rev.* Suppl. **68**, Ejnaar Munksgaard, Copenhagen.

Craik, K. J. W. (1947). "Theory of Human Operator in Control Systems: (1) The Operator as an Engineering System", *Br. J. Psychol.* **38**, 56.

Craik, K. J. W. (1948). "Theory of Human Operator in Control Systems: (2) Man as an Element in a Control System", *Br. J. Psychol.* **38**, 142.

Darwin, C. (1873). "The Expression of the Emotions in Man and Animals", Appleton, New York.

Delay, J. (1942). "Les Dissolutions de la mémoire", Presses Univ. de France, Paris.

Delay, J., Pichot, P., Nicholas-Charles, P., and Perse, J. (1959). Étude psychométrique des effets de l'amo-barbital (amytal) et de la chlorpromazine sur des sujets normaux. *Psychopharmocologia* **1**, 48–58.

Eccles, J. C. (1966). "Brain and Conscious Experience" (Final Discussion), Springer-Verlag, Berlin, Heidelberg and New York.

Eysenck, H. J. (1960). "The Structure of Human Personalities", Methuen, London.

Fenichel, O. (1953). " The Collected Papers", First series. W. W. Norton, New York.

Fessard, A. E. (1954). "Mechanisms of Nervous Integration and Conscious Experience", *In* "Brain Mechanisms and Consciousness" (Delafresnaye, J. F., ed.), Blackwell Scientific Publications, Oxford.

Fisher, R. A. (1938). "Statistical Methods for Research Workers", Oliver and Boyd, Edinburgh.

Fraisse, P. (1964). "The Psychology of Time", Eyre and Spottiswoode, London.

Freeman, G. L. (1939). "The Problem of Set", *Am. J. Psychol.* **52**, 16–30.

Freeman, G. L. (1940). "Discussion: 'Central' *vs* 'Peripheral' Locus of Set; a Critique of the Mowrer, Rayman and Bliss 'demonstration' ". *J. exp. Psychol.* **26**, 622–628.

Freeman, G. L. (1948). "Physiological Psychology", Van Nostrand, New York.

Freud, S. (1936). "The Problem of Anxiety", W. W. Norton, New York.

Fulton, J. F. (1955). "Textbook of Physiology", Saunders, Philadelphia.

Garner, W. R. (1962). "Uncertainty and Structure as Psychological Concept", John Wiley and Sons Inc., New York and London.

Goldman-Eisler, F. (1951). "The Measurement of Time Sequences in Conversational Behaviour", *Br. J. Psychol.* Gen. Sec. **42**, 355–362.

Goldman-Eisler, F. (1952). "Individual Differences between Interviewers and their Effects on Interviewees' Conversational Behaviour", *J. ment. Sci.* **98**, 660–671.

Goldman-Eisler, F. (1954). "On the Variability of the Speed of Talking and on its Relation to the Length of Utterance in Conversation", *Br. J. Psychol.* Gen. Sec. **45**, 94–107.

Goldman-Eisler, F. (1955). "Speech-Breathing Activity—A Measure of Tension and Affect during Interviews", *Br. J. Psychol.* Gen. Sec. 53–63.

Goldman-Eisler, F. (1956a). "Speech-Breathing Activity and Context in Psychiatric Interviews", *Br. J. Psychol.* Med. Sec. **29**, 35–48.

Goldman-Eisler, F. (1956b). "A Contribution to the Objective Measurement of the Cathartic Process", *J. ment. Sci.* **102**, 78–95.

Goldman-Eisler, F. (1956c). "The Determinants of the Rate of Speech and their Mutual Relations", *J. psychosom. Res.* **2**, 137–143.

Goldman-Eisler, F. (1957). "Speech Production and Language Statistics", *Nature, Lond.* **180**, 1497.

Goldman-Eisler, F. (1958a). "Speech Analysis and Mental Processes", *Language and Speech* **I**, 59–75.

Goldman-Eisler, F. (1958b). "Speech Production and the Predictability of Words in Context", *Q. J. exp. Psychol.* Vol. 10, 96–106

Goldman-Eisler, F. (1958c). "The Predictability of Words in Context and the Length of Pauses in Speech", *Language and Speech*, **I**, Part 3, 226–231.

Goldman-Eisler, F. (1961a). "The Significance of Changes in the Rate of Articulation", *Language and Speech*, **4**, Part 3, 171–174.

Goldman-Eisler, F. (1961b). "The Continuity of Speech Utterance, its Determinants and its Significance", *Language and Speech*, **4**, 220–231.

Goldman-Eisler, F. (1961c). "The Distribution of Pause Durations in Speech", *Language and Speech*, **4**, 232–237.

Goldman-Eisler, F. (1961d). "Hesitation and Information in Speech", *In* "Information Theory" (Colin Cherry, ed.), Butterworth, London.

Goldman-Eisler, F. (1961e), "A Comparative Study of Two Hesitation Phenomena", *Language and Speech*, **4**, Part 1, 18–26.

Goldman-Eisler, F. (1964). "Language and the Science of Man (Discussion and Further Comments)", *In* "New Directions in the Study of Language", 8–22 (E. H. Lenneberg, ed.), M.I.T. Press, Cambridge, Mass. U.S.A.

Goldman-Eisler, F. (1964). "Hesitation, Information and Levels of Speech Production", *In* "Disorders of Language" (A. V. S. de Reuck and Maeve O'Connor, eds.), Ciba Foundation Symposium, J. and A. Churchill Ltd, London.

Goldman-Eisler, F., and Mendoza, R. (1965). "Automatic Pause-time Recording, Counting and Totalising Equipment" (Distributed by) The Clearinghouse for Federal and Scientific Information, U.S. Department of Commerce/National Bureau of Standards/Institute of Applied Technology.

Goldman-Eisler, F., Skarbek, A., and Henderson, A. (1965a). "The Effect of Chlorpromazine on Speech Behaviour", *Psychopharmacologia* **7**, 220–229.

Goldman-Eisler, F., Skarbek, A., and Henderson, A. (1965b). "Cognitive and Neurochemical Determination of Sentence Structure", *Language and Speech* **8**, 86–94.

Goldman-Eisler, F., Skarbek, A., and Henderson A. (1966). "Breath Rate and the Selective Action of Chlorpromazine on Speech Behaviour", *Psychopharmacologia* **8**, 415–427.

Goldman-Eisler, F. (1967). "Sequential Temporal Patterns and Cognitive Processes in Speech", *Language and Speech* **10**, 122–132.

Goldman-Eisler, F., Skarbek, A., and Henderson, A. (1967). "The Effect of Chlorpromazine on the Control of Speech-Breathing Mechanisms", *J. Verbal Learning and Verbal Behaviour* **6**, No. 1, 73–77.

Goldstein, K. (1948). "Language and Language Disturbances", Grune and Stratton, New York.

Golla, F.L. (1921). "The Objective Study of Neurosis", *Lancet* II, 115–122.

Golla, F. L., and Antonovitch, B. S. (1929). "The Respiratory Rhythm in its Relation to the Mechanism of Thought", *Brain* **52**, 491–509.

Haldane, J. S., and Priestley, J. G. (1935). "Respiration", Oxford at The Clarendon Press.

Harnik, J. (1930). "One Component of the Fear of Death in Early Infancy", *Int. J. Psycho-Analysis* XI, 485–499.

Head, H. (1926). "Aphasia and Kindred Disorders of Speech", 2 vols, Cambridge University Press, London.

Hebb, D. O. (1949). "The Organisation of Behavior: A Neurophysiological Theory", Wiley, New York.

Henderson, A., Goldman-Eisler, F., and Skarbek, A. (1965). "The Common Value of Pausing Time in Spontaneous Speech", *Q.J. exp. Psychol.* **17**, 343–345.

Henderson, A., Goldman-Eisler, F., and Skarbek, A. (1966a). "Temporal Patterns of Cognitive Activity and Breath Control in Speech", *Language and Speech* **8**, Part 4, 236–242.

Henderson, A., Goldman-Eisler, F., and Skarbek, A. (1966b). "Sequential Temporal Patterns in Spontaneous Speech", *Language and Speech* **9**, 207–216.

Henze, R. (1953). "Experimentelle Untersuchungen zur Phänomenologie der Sprechgeschwindigkeit", *Z. exp. angew. Psychol.* **2**, 214–243.

Herdan, G. (1960). "Language as Choice and Chance", Noordhoff, Groningen.

Ichlondsky, N. E. (1930). "Neuropsyche und Hirnrinde", Vol. II, Chapter IV. *Physiologische Grundlagen der Tiefenpsychologie*, Urban Schwarzenberg, Vienna-Berlin.

Jackson, H. J. (1878). "On Affections of Speech from Disease of the Brain", reprinted in "Selected Writings of Hughlings Jackson" (1958). Vol. II, pp. 155–170, Basic Books, New York.

James, W. (1890). "The Principles of Psychology", Macmillan and Co., London.

Jones, R. E. (1949). "Personality Changes in Psychotics following Prefrontal Lobotomy", *J. abnorm. soc. Psychol.* **44**, 315–328.

Judson, L. S. V. and Weaver, A. T. (1966). "Voice Science", Vision Press Limited, London.

Kainz, Friedrich (1954). "Psychologie der Sprache" III Bd., Ferdinand Enke Verlag, Stuttgart.

Katz, J. J., and Fodor, J. A. (1964). "The Structure of a Semantic Theory", *In* "Readings in the Philosophy of Language" (J. A. Fodor and J. J. Katz, eds.), Prentice-Hall Inc., Englewood Cliffs, New Jersey.

Kubie, L. S. (1948). "Instinct and Homeostasis", *J. psychosom. Med.* **10**, 15–30.

Ladefoged, P., Draper, M. H., and Whitterage, D. (1958). "Syllables and Stress", *Miscellanea Phonetica* III, 1–14.

Lashley, K. S. (1951). "The Problem of Serial Order in Behavior", *In* "Cerebral Mechanisms in Behaviour", The Hixon Symposium (L. A. Jeffres, ed.) John Wiley and Sons, New York and London.

Lenneberg, E. H. (1966). "Speech Development: Its Anatomical and Physiological Concomitants", *Brain Function*, Vol. III, Proceedings of the Third Conference, 1963. "Speech, Language and Communication" (E. C. Corterett, ed.), University of California Press, Berkeley and Los Angeles, California.

Lounsbury, F. G. (1954). "Pausal, Juncture and Hesitation Phenomena", *In* "Psycholinguistics: A Survey of Theory and Research Problems", C. E. Osgood and T. A. Sebeok, eds, Supplement to *J. abnorm. sec. Psychol.*, Baltimore.

Luria, A. R. (1961). "The Role of Speech in the Regulation of Normal and Abnormal Behaviour", Pergamon Press, Oxford, London.

Luria, A. R. (1966). "Higher Cortical Functions in Man", Tavistock Publications, London.

Markoff, A. A. (1913). "Essai d'une Récherche Statistique sur le Texte du Roman 'Eugene Onegin' ", *Bull. Acad. Imper. Sci.*, St. Petersburg VII.

Merleau-Ponty, M. (1965). "The Structure of Behaviour", Methuen, London.

Miller, G. A. (1951). "Language and Communication", McGraw-Hill Book Co. Inc., New York, Toronto, London.

Miller, G. A. (1964). "Communication and the Structure of Behavior", *In* "Disorders of Communication", Proceedings for Research and Mental Disease (D. McK. Rioch and E. A. Weinstein, eds), The Williams and Wilkins Co., Baltimore.

Miller, G. A., Galanter, E., and Pribram, K. (1960). "Plans and the Structure of Behavior", Holt, Rinehart and Winston, Inc., New York.

Mowrer, O. H. (1950). "Learning Theory and the Symbolic Processes", John Wiley and Sons Ltd, New York.

Pike, K. L. (1958). "Phonetics: A Critical Analysis of Phonetic Theory and a Technique for the Practical Description of Sounds", *Language and Literature*, Vol. XXI, University of Michigan Press, Ann Arbor, Michigan.

Porot, M. (1947). "La Leucotomie préfrontale au psychiatrie", *Annls méd.-psychol.* **105**, 121–142.

Pribram, K. (1962). "Interrelations of Psychology and the Neurological Disciplines", *In* "Psychology: A Study of Science", Vol. 4, McGraw-Hill Book Co. Inc., New York, London.

Ramsay, R. W. (1966). "Personality and Speech", *J. Pers. Soc. Psychol.* **4**, 116–118.

Schilling, R. (1929). Über "Inneres Sprechen", *Z. Psychol.* III, 204–255.

Shannon, C. E. (1951). "Prediction and Entropy of Printed English", *The Bell System Tech. J.* **30**.

Skarbek, A. (1967). "The Significance of Variations in Breathing Behaviour in Speech and at Rest". Ph.D. Thesis, London University.

Stetson, R. H. (1928). "Motor Phonetics: A Study of Speech Movement in Action", *Arch. Neerl. Phon. Exp.* III, 1–216.

Suter, J. (1912). "Die Beziehung zwischen Aufmerksamkeit und Atmung", *Arch. ges. Psychol.* XXV, 78–150.

Vygotsky, L. S. (1962). "Thought and Language", M.I.T. Press, Massachusetts Inst. of Technology and John Wiley and Sons Inc., New York and London.

Author Index

The page numbers in italics refer to the entries in full in the References.

163

Subject Index